Writing a Successful Research Paper

A Simple Approach

Writing a Successful Research Paper

A Simple Approach

Stanley Chodorow

Hackett Publishing Company, Inc.
Indianapolis/Cambridge

15 14 13 12 11   1 2 3 4 5 6 7

For further information, please address
    Hackett Publishing Company, Inc.
    P.O. Box 44937
    Indianapolis, Indiana 46244-0937

    www.hackettpublishing.com

Cover design by Brian Rak
Interior design and composition by Mary Vasquez
Printed at Edwards Brothers, Inc.

Library of Congress Cataloging-in-Publication Data
Chodorow, Stanley.
 Writing a successful research paper : a simple approach / Stanley
Chodorow.
    p. cm.
 Includes bibliographical references and index.
 ISBN 978-1-60384-440-6 (pbk.) – ISBN 978-1-60384-441-3
(cloth)
  1. English language–Rhetoric. 2. Report writing. 3. Academic
writing. I. Title.
 PE1408.C4727 2011
 808'.042–dc23
               2011024035

Contents

Preface

This guide stems from my experience participating in and reflecting on a general education program for first- and second-year undergraduates in which I taught for many years at the University of California, San Diego. The strategic approach of that program gave me a new perspective on my long previous experience of teaching undergraduate and graduate students to write papers. As a historian I had not self-consciously focused on teaching students how to choose topics, do research, and construct an argument. The writing program of the Making of the Modern World (MMW) sequence of the Eleanor Roosevelt College at the University of California, San Diego provided a framework for teaching students how to do these things and more. I quickly noticed that students in upper-division courses who had gone through the program had a big advantage over other students when taking on the typical paper assignments of courses in their majors.

MMW is a two-year core sequence that covers world history and civilizations from the evolution of human beings to the present. Faculty members and graduate students from nearly all the departments in the humanities and social sciences teach the courses, so paper assignments come from a wide range of disciplinary perspectives and interests. In its second and third terms, the sequence incorporates an intensive writing program. For me, the systematic approach of this program brought together all of the disparate pieces of advice and guidance I had been giving students for decades and made writing this guide possible.

I want to acknowledge the contributions of Jackie Giordano, who has for many years been the coordinator of the intensive writing program in MMW. During the seven years we worked together, I came to believe that the program should be made available to students in other colleges and universities. Jackie and I started working on the guide together, but her many commitments made it impossible for her to take responsibility for co-writing it. Nonetheless, she gave me an understanding of the principles on which the program rested, and I consulted with her in the early stages of writing. She provided the Rough Draft Worksheet (Chapter 8) and the idea for the Argument Chart (Chapter 5). She also suggested, in a different form, the classification of questions offered in Chapter 3, an important element in determining what kinds of questions are suitable for research papers. I am deeply grateful to her.

I have benefited from the insights of Matthew Herbst, the Director of MMW, and Heidi Keller-Lapp, who is responsible for managing the second year of the sequence. The anonymous readers who reviewed the draft for Hackett helped me broaden the disciplinary reach of the guide, and one reader, Joel Relihan, who went through the text with the eye of an editor, caught many awkward or unclear passages and made telling remarks on where certain points should be made. I benefited a lot from the readers' criticisms and suggestions. I also benefited immensely from the careful work done by Brian Rak, the editor in charge of the book for Hackett. He did the kind of job one used to see in academic publishing but that is rare now. I appreciate his penetrating questions and editorial hand. I also appreciate the work of the copyeditor, Harbour Fraser Hodder, who improved the text in many ways. Finally, I want to thank production editor Mary Vasquez, who wrestled the text into book form and displayed great patience in accommodating second thoughts.

My son Adam, a professor of law and frequent recipient of my editorial suggestions, read a draft of the guide and made valuable suggestions of his own; turnabout is fair play. Finally, my wife Peggy read a draft, and, as she did when she read my dissertation decades ago, brought her outsider's sensibility to bear on my prose and on the organization of my presentation. There's magic in the combination of criticism and encouragement she delivers.

Stanley Chodorow
La Jolla, California

Introduction

Writing a Research Paper

Students often regard the assignment of writing a research paper as a daunting task. Even if they have written such papers in high school, they know that more is expected of them in college and that the standard they must meet will be higher. This guide aims to show students that if they break down the process and carry it out in steps, they can master the required tasks and complete the assignment successfully.

The best way to use this guide is to read it through before you start work on the paper. Then you will have an overview of the steps you must take to complete the paper successfully, and you will be able to return to specific chapters easily as you work.

In all fields of knowledge, the aim of research is to answer a question. Scientists do experiments or make observations to answer questions. Humanists and social scientists do research in libraries and museums or in the field by assembling and analyzing data in order to answer questions. The techniques and settings for the research may differ from one academic discipline to another and one project to another, but the basic intellectual process is the same. The skills you develop when you learn to do research and write papers will serve you in any course you take in college.

Writing a research paper is actually pretty straightforward and simple. It involves intellectual skills that nearly everyone uses every day. We frequently make statements or give answers to questions that someone challenges, and so we frequently defend ourselves by making arguments based on evidence. The aim is to persuade someone—a parent, teacher, coach, or friend—that your statement was true or your answer to a question was good and sufficient. Examples of such exchanges range from the trivial to the serious, from defending the statement that Michael Jordan was the greatest basketball player ever to defending the assertion that the only way to reform health care is to institute a single-payer system.

When doing a research paper, you proceed as you do in informal exchanges, but you do it systematically. You answer a question (one you have formulated or that your teacher has given to you) and support your answer with an argument based on evidence that you have found through research. You use counterarguments to test the quality of your evidence and argument. You want your reader to accept your answer as right, or at least as plausible and interesting; even if you cannot prove that you are right, you want your reader to admit that you've made a good case. This guide will help you develop skills you already have so that you can complete a research paper without all the anxiety that paper assignments so often generate.

While writing a research paper requires time and effort, there's nothing mysterious about it. It's just another task—actually, a series of tasks. You have an assignment with a due date; you have a series of discrete tasks to complete. The work is not difficult, and it can be great fun. But doing the work requires a plan of action and the discipline to carry it out. This guide gives you the plan. You supply the discipline.

Typically, we distinguish two types of undergraduate papers: essays and research (or term) papers. When a teacher asks you to write a paper based on a question about a text assigned in the course, she is asking you to write an essay. When the paper assignment requires you to use resources that *you* have identified—original documents, data sets, works of art, scholarly works—the project is a research paper. In introductory courses, paper assignments nearly always ask you to write essays.

Yet essay assignments always require you to formulate a thesis (an answer to the question posed in the assignment) and to support that thesis with an argument. Essay questions on exams require the same things. Seen in this way, an essay is the simplest kind of research paper. You do not have to find sources; they are given to you. However, you should approach the source(s) in the same way you would if you had done three weeks of work gathering them. You read the source material carefully; come up with a thesis; choose passages or data from the source(s) to support your argument that your thesis is a good one; find other passages or data that seem to undermine your argument; and counter the counterargument to show that your choice of evidence and your interpretation of it is best. Note that you are not required to prove your thesis. (Ordinarily, good paper topics do not have definitive answers.) Your job is to propose a good answer supported by a good argument based on a reasonable interpretation of the evidence you have found.

Above the introductory level, assignments often require you to find your own topic, specifying only that it be relevant to the subject of the course. Formulating a suitable question is often a challenge, so this guide takes you through the process of doing that. It also gives you advice about taking notes on what you read, on organizing what you discover through research, and on constructing an argument.

In fact, this guide takes you through the whole process of writing a research paper. In addition to this guide, however, you may find it helpful to refer to other types of guides that include either more detailed or more general information about specific components of research, writing, and argument. There are many, and the publisher of this guide offers several: Although *Writing a Successful Research Paper: A Simple Approach* discusses the nature, types, use, and misuse of sources, Gordon Harvey's *Writing with Sources: A Guide for Students,* Second Edition (Hackett Publishing Company, 2008), provides styles of documentation and a fuller treatment of methods. My guide discusses the types and uses of argument and evidence in research papers in Chapters 5 and 6; for clear and practical guidance on the art of critical thinking in general, see Anthony Weston's *A Rulebook for Arguments,* Fourth Edition (Hackett Publishing Company, 2008). The last chapter of my guide provides a few pointers on writing style, but for comprehensive guidance you should consult a composition handbook. Such handbooks cover grammar, usage, sentence and paragraph structure, and related topics. There are many excellent ones to choose from, and you may have one from your first college composition course.

But back to our topic. What are the characteristics of a good research paper? To answer this question you first have to understand the nature of academic writing.

Academic writing has two characteristics not usually present in other types of writing such as journalism or creative writing.

First, the academic writer situates his or her question and argument in the history of scholarship on the subject. Citing other scholars and acknowledging their contribution, even if you disagree with their ideas, is a critical element of academic writing. Second, academic writers expose the sources of the evidence they use. It is not enough to cite evidence; you also have to explain where the evidence comes from and how it was produced or collected. Your reader needs to be persuaded that the evidence you use comes from reliable sources and represents what you claim it does. Journalists cite sources, but they do not ordinarily use their precious column inches to discuss the quality of their sources; academic writers have to do that. This guide will teach you about the proper use of other writers' work and how to assess the quality of evidence and its sources.

Beyond these basic characteristics, the quality of a paper depends on the quality of its specific components: the formulation of the question posed; the formulation of the proposed answer (or thesis); the argument made to support the thesis; the research done to find both evidence that supports the thesis as well as earlier scholarship that at least touched on your topic and evidence; the persuasive use of the evidence; the writing itself; and the care taken in making the text presentable (spelling, punctuation, etc.). In a good paper, you present your ideas based on your interpretation of the evidence. You cannot accomplish this by stringing together quotations from your sources. If you do that, you are merely handing in selections from what you've read, and the instructor will ask, "But what do *you* think about the subject?" An excellent paper has a sound thesis and a strong argument that demonstrates that you have done a substantial amount of work.

When an assignment asks you to choose a topic and write a paper on it, you need a work plan. That plan starts with the identification of a broadly defined research area or topic from which you will select a specific subject that interests you and that meets the requirements of the assignment. You narrow the focus of your topic to the appropriate scope by looking for a specific topic within that general one. After choosing a general research topic, you begin reading relevant scholarly works. In a process described in Chapter 1, you look for a topic suitable to the length of the paper you have to write and to the amount of time you have to do it. Reading critically is crucial to defining a topic and to working efficiently, and Chapter 2 gives you some guidance in that set of skills. The reading process leads to the formulation of a research question, which is covered in Chapter 3.

Once you've reached this stage, your research becomes focused on finding the evidence needed to answer the question and on scholarly works in which the authors tried to answer the question or part of it. As you proceed with this work, you will usually revise your question in response to what you discover. Chapter 4 deals with this process of refinement. Then you write a tentative answer to your question (a working thesis) and start to construct an argument and line up the evidence behind it. Chapter 5 guides you through this stage of the work. Chapter 6 deals with the questions regarding evidence: "What counts as sound evidence?" "What's the best way to use evidence?" and "When do you have enough evidence?" Chapter 7 discusses the ways one credits sources and the reasons why one does so. When you have constructed your argument, you are ready to write a first draft of the paper. Chapter 8 gives you a rough draft worksheet and advice about this initial stage of writing. Chapters 9 and 10 take you through the processes of revising the rough draft and then polishing the paper for submission.

You will be writing research or term papers under significant time pressure. This guide will help you stay on schedule and do each task in as orderly a way as possible in the usually messy and chaotic environment of an academic term. So there's no time to waste—let's get going.

Synopsis of the Research and Writing Process

Begin work on your assignment as soon as you receive it.

1. **Find a research topic.** Start with a broad topic within which you will expect to find the narrow topic for your paper. (Chapter 1)

2. **Start reading** articles, books, and reviews of those books on this broad topic. As you read, note (in writing) the narrower topics that particularly intrigue you and all questions that occur to you about these topics. (Book reviews will point out controversial points or faulty arguments in the literature, as will some articles, if their authors respond to the work of others.) Take notes as you read. When you find texts relevant to your topic, photocopy them or print them out. Record the complete citation information for each text. (Chapter 2)

3. **Formulate an open-ended question and write it down.** Stop reading and consider what you have found. Look over all of the texts and notes you have accumulated. You will see several possible topics; choose one or two to read more about. When you have settled on a topic, formulate an open-ended question that you would like to answer in your research paper. This question will focus your work, which now aims to answer the question. (Chapter 3)

4. **Return to reading.** This time, focus on texts or data or works of art that provide information directly relevant to your research question. As before, photocopy or print out relevant sources, with complete citation information. Annotate the relevant parts of each text, data set, or artwork. When you have learned enough about your topic that you start to

feel burdened by the weight of information, stop and reflect on what you have learned. Write some pages of notes and commentary on your ideas. Try to note all potential answers to your research question. If you find that your research is not pointing you toward an answer to your original question, revise or sharpen your question. This recursive process of reading, reflecting, and sharpening your question is a cycle that should be repeated for as long as time permits. Continue to read, reflect, and sharpen your question until you need to move on to the writing of a rough draft. (Chapter 4)

5. **Write down a tentative answer to your research question.** Your tentative answer is your working thesis. Sort all of your notes, commentaries, photocopies, and so forth by subtopic or category of evidence. Arrange the categories in the order that will be most effective for arguing your thesis. When you have put your evidence in order, you have the skeleton of your argument. Assess whether you have enough evidence to support your argument. (Chapters 5–6)

6. **Write a complete rough draft,** including a Works Cited page (or pages), that answers your research question by integrating all the results of your research, including your summaries, notes, and reflections. If you have not already studied the style sheet that many instructors hand out as part of the paper assignment, do so before you start writing your first draft. The style sheet specifies how you should cite references, present your bibliography, set your margins, etc. You could lose grade points if you do not follow the specified style. (Chapters 7–8)

7. **Revise your rough draft.** Print out your rough draft and put it away for a while (or turn it in, if you are required to do so). After a few days, thoroughly revise the draft for organization, clarity, and explanation of evidence. Delete unnecessary sections. Note where you need to add more evidence or explanation. Where necessary, do more research and provide more support for the weaker parts of your argument. If your instructor or peers have commented on your rough draft, make sure to incorporate or at least deal with their suggestions as you revise the draft. Make sure that you have

cited all of your sources and that your Works Cited page is complete. (Chapter 9)

8. **Copyedit and prepare a final revision.** A day or so before the paper is due, revise your paper for spelling, punctuation, grammar, and other sentence-level concerns. It often helps to read the paper aloud, which can help you identify awkward sentences and misused words. Note also that spell-checkers in computer programs will not highlight words that are in the dictionary but are the wrong words in context. Print out the paper. Give it one last reading to make sure that everything is correct. (Chapter 10)

Chapter 1

Finding a Research Question and the Resources to Write about It

Getting Started—Choosing a General Topic

For various reasons, many students see the choice of a topic as a big obstacle. It is true that the choice of a good topic is extremely important, but the task isn't so daunting when approached systematically, and it should certainly not be paralyzing.

Some students find it difficult to imagine a topic that might serve them well because they do not see the possibilities, many of them right under their noses. When the teacher leaves it to you to find a topic, you have the opportunity to write on a fairly wide range of subjects. In a history course, you must write on the region (Europe, the United States, China, etc.) and period (ancient, early modern, modern, etc.) covered by the course, but you could focus on economic, political, intellectual, cultural, or social history, and within each of these categories you have many choices. In a sociology course focused on the family, you can write about relations among families or sibling rivalries, or the behavior of families in different economic situations, or families and religion. In literature, music history, or art history, you will have a wide choice of works, artists, movements, and themes to study. Paper assignments—at least those above the introductory level—are not like exams. They don't require you to answer someone else's questions but rather give you an opportunity to define a topic and answer a question of your own. In that way, they are liberating. Yet this liberty creates anxiety in some students precisely because there are so many possibilities to choose from. How to choose?

Start looking for a topic by thinking about your own interests. Are you interested in economics? Consider questions about the economics of a period, a region, an institution, even about how a literary author portrays or uses economics in a story. Interested in biology? The role of disease or medical practices and beliefs might provide a good topic. Be assured that in humanities and social science courses, you will have many opportunities to pursue your particular interests.

A textbook can be a good place to start your search for a general topic. Peruse the chapter and subchapter headings. When you find something that interests you, read it and see if the author's bibliography can direct you to other works that would deepen your knowledge of the subject. When you have a general idea of what might interest you, look in the library's subject catalog for titles that seem relevant and interesting. (There will be more on using the library later in this chapter.)

The general topic should be broad enough to allow you to read a variety of interesting materials, yet not so broad as to be vague or amorphous. For a 10-page research paper, a topic such as "the rise of the middle class," with no specification of the society or period in question, would be much too broad to guide you in your initial reading. Specifying the period and place— "the rise of the middle class in England in the 18th century"— would allow you to start reading. (Later you would select some narrower aspect of this topic to focus on, and the final topic would have to be quite focused. If, for example, you were interested in middle-class women, a topic such as "women in the 18th century" would still be too broad for a final topic, so you would have to narrow your focus to a topic such as the education of 18th-century English women, or their role in education, or their role in the English economy, or their legal rights, and so forth.) Similarly, a topic such as "childhood" would not give you sufficient guidance about where to start and what to read. Specifying where and when would help, but in order to achieve an appropriately broad, general topic, you would have to focus on some aspect of childhood—"the concept of childhood in West Africa" (anthropology or sociology), perhaps, or "the education of children in early 19th-century England" (history or English). An appropriately broad topic suggests a bibliography and a section of the library to search.

Just as unhelpful as a topic that is too broad, a topic that is too narrow might lead you to a very small shelf; little if anything might have been written about it. You will find little scholarship on "the place of puppet theater in contemporary Cambodian society," even if you read Khmer, French, or Japanese. By choosing a broad general topic, you maximize your chance of finding something interesting, feasible, and substantial to work on.

Here are some examples of good, appropriately broad, general topics in a few different disciplines:

In history:
> Women in the Reformation
> New technology and social change in the Industrial Revolution
> Economic change in T'ang Dynasty China

In sociology:
> Social class and race in American cities
> Church communities and social class
> Educational performance and family background

In literature:
> Short stories published in *The Atlantic Monthly* during the 1920s and 1930s
> British novels about seafaring in the mid-19th century
> Images of women in the literature of the Progressive Era in America

In art history:
> The influence of European styles on Native American rug design in the 19th century
> Roman funerary art
> Art and theories of light in 17th-century Dutch painting

In anthropology:
> Food customs in Amazonian culture
> The role of law in tribal society
> The survival of traditional religious beliefs in societies recently converted to Christianity or Islam

In political science:
> Voting patterns among U.S. working-class women
> Courts and institutional change in constitutional systems
> Lobbying and legislation on food safety

Remember: You are looking for a topic that interests you and meets the criteria that the instructor set in the assignment. You may think that if you are taking a course in your major or you are a non-major who has chosen to take the course, this advice is superfluous; you are already interested in the subject. However, the topic of a paper is much more specific than the topic of a course. To find a topic, start from your disciplinary or subject-area interests—science, engineering, literature, visual art, law, etc.—and consider what general topics relating to your interests fit the course you are taking. You will do your best work when you work on topics that reflect your interests.

Gathering Information on Your Broad, General Topic

When you have an idea about what general topic you wish to work on, you should begin gathering information on it. Today, many people start looking for information on the Internet. However, the Internet has drawbacks as a source. First, most of the material on the Internet is in short articles, which will not give you enough information to lead to the next stage of your reading. For example, Wikipedia articles tend to be brief and focused on specific subjects. (Moreover, you don't know the identity of the authors or anything about their credibility, and the articles often contain incorrect or partial information.) Thus, starting your research on the Internet might provide you with some very basic information about some aspects of your topic, but using only the Internet will often give you a fragmented body of information of uncertain accuracy or value.

Finding a recent general book on your topic and mining it for information is the best strategy for getting started. You can find such a book by looking at the reviews in the major scholarly journal of the discipline you are working in, such as the *American Sociological Review*, the *American Political Science Review*, and the *American Economic Review*. Your instructor or a reference librarian can tell you which journals would be most useful. Book reviews will tell you whether scholars in the discipline think a book is a good survey of a field or topic and often will give you some insight into the book's take on a subject. If the reviewer notes that the author advances a particular interpretation of an issue he or she covers, consider the interpretation itself as a topic for your paper. A difference of opinion about a subject implies at least the general question, "What is it about the evidence on that subject that permits different conclusions to be drawn from it?" A book review might indicate a number of narrow questions to be considered.

A general book will give you basic information about your subject. In art history, the book will introduce you to the major artists of a period or movement, provide some illustrations of their work, and characterize their interests, styles, and so on. In anthropology, the book will tell you which aspects of which societies have been studied and what scholars have concluded from these studies. In economics, the work might tell you what theories have been proposed, how scholars have built models to test them, and what data is available for you to use. The authors of general works of scholarship will have organized the material into a coherent narrative or analysis from which you can get a grasp of the subject as a whole, and they will have done a lot of scholarly work for you.

First, the bibliography will be a trove of resources for your project. Just reading the titles of the works the author used will provide you with suggestions about where to look next. Second, pay attention to the footnotes; you may find your topic in one of them, because authors often use footnotes to discuss a scholarly controversy over the interpretation of evidence or to reject another scholar's thesis. Third, don't ignore the table of contents or index (especially if it is a subject index); both can help you find a topic by showing how an author has structured her research as well as by revealing considerations her research has taken into account and suggesting others it might have neglected. Finally, the author will point you to the evidence on the subject and where it can be found.

Finding Your Narrow, Specific Topic

Your job at this stage is to find a relatively narrow, specific topic within the broad general topic that interests you. A big topic includes many smaller topics, and as you read you should be looking for subtopics that catch your eye. The thing about a topic most likely to catch your attention is a question it raises. The author may write something that does not satisfy you, prompting a question of your own; or you may find that two authors disagree on the answer to a previously posed question. (As noted, the controversy might be revealed in a footnote rather than in the text.) When a question occurs to you or you get an urge to know more, you have an opening to a potential topic for your paper. You will find that questions occur to you at critical points in a scholar's work—places where the author explicitly disagrees with another scholar (which indicates that the point is controversial); places where the author changes direction (usually by using words like "however," "but," and "although"); and places where you think the evidence cited to support a point doesn't really do so.

In looking for a specific topic for your paper, then, you are looking not just for a topic but for a question about it. You may be interested in a suitably narrow topic and want to read about it, but you do not have the basis for a research paper until you have a question you want to answer. You do research not just to collect information but to advance a position or thesis, which is the answer to a question; the question must come first. Chapter 3 will introduce you to different types of questions, but for now, note that you are looking for a question that you can't answer by simply looking in a reference book or Wikipedia. A question such as, "When was Abraham Lincoln elected to the Illinois Legislature?" is of no use; you can answer it by looking in an encyclopedia. You are looking for a question that cannot be answered so simply or definitively, such as "What did Lincoln hope to accomplish in the Gettysburg Address?" That question will take you to the text of the Address itself; to what we know about how and when Lincoln wrote it; to why he thought it important to go to Gettysburg to deliver the speech; to questions about why he made it so short when his contemporaries were in the habit of giving speeches that lasted for hours; and so forth. On this topic, and its subtopics, you'll find a great deal of scholarly work and many different opinions. This kind of open-ended question is perfect for a research paper.

Evidence and Sources of Evidence

Once you have a question, you need to find information that will help you answer it: you are looking for sources. They come in two types. The first is scholarship, which is the type you used when trying to formulate your question. Scholars do what you are doing: they formulate questions; find evidence that they can use to answer the questions; and construct arguments, based on evidence, that support the answers they want to give. However, scholarly opinion is not evidence; you cannot cite a scholar's opinion to prove a point you want to make. But you *can* cite it to show that you are not alone in the way you interpret the evidence or to show, by disagreeing with a scholar's view, that you have taken an independent position. For you, scholarship will most often provide guidance to the evidence you need and interpretations of the evidence that you can use in creating your own interpretation. (There will be more on evidence and interpretation in Chapter 6.)

The second and more important type of source consists of or offers evidence about your topic. **Evidence is data or information used to support a claim**. Usually, the actors, authors, or institutions whose actions, works, or character you wish to explain will have produced the evidence. (It may also have been produced by scholars who have collected data, such as surveys of public opinion, on your subject.) Evidence thus comes in many types: in literature, it most often consists of passages from the works you are writing about; in art history, works of art and the writings of and interviews with artists; in economics, data such as that produced by government agencies (the U.S. Census Bureau, the U.S. Commerce Department, the World Bank, etc.); in history, documents, writings, and artworks produced by the people of the time and place you are studying. In some fields, such as sociology and political science, you might collect your own evidence by doing a survey of your fellow students or by interviewing a number of them, but you might also use existing survey results published or available through a social science databank.

The usual terms for the two types of sources are "primary" and "secondary." **Primary sources consist of or contain the evidence you use in your argument. Secondary sources are scholarly works that refer to, explain, and interpret evidence and its sources.**

In some fields, such as anthropology and some areas of sociology, using primary sources directly may be impractical because you cannot spend months living in a foreign society, interviewing its members, and observing their lives. In such cases, the notes and transcripts, descriptions, and recordings of events and performances that scholars have made during their work in the field could be considered primary sources, while the interpretation offered by the observer, surveyor, or interviewer could be considered secondary sources. However, in these disciplines the author of the secondary source is often actually a participant in the creation of the "primary" sources, and the field notes and other "raw" materials are only rarely available to others. When you are working in a field that relies on participant-observer techniques, you have to focus on the way the data was collected, assembled, and used by the author as well as on the data itself.

In such fields, where the true primary materials (field notes, etc.) are not available, assignments for research papers typically ask you to assess the scholarship on a subject, and in such assignments secondary sources become your primary sources. You will make arguments that rest on what scholars have written and on the way they have used the evidence they collected in their fieldwork. For example, in 1928 Margaret Mead published a study of Samoan society (*Coming of Age in Samoa*) that became a major work in anthropology. The book was immediately controversial with the reading public because it portrayed a society with sexual mores fundamentally different from those in Western societies and, as many Western Europeans and Americans saw it, at odds with morally acceptable relations between the sexes. Some anthropologists also criticized the work, but it was not until 1983 that Derek Freeman published a thorough analysis and critique of the work, challenging its authority as a sound work of anthropological scholarship and setting off a controversy that reverberated well beyond the discipline of anthropology. A paper on this controversy would take the views of Mead, Freeman, and others as evidence and use their works as primary sources.

Anthropology is not the only discipline in which paper assignments require students to review the scholarly literature on a topic. Such assignments are common in both introductory and upper-level courses in all disciplines. But how do these papers relate to those in which you use raw evidence collected out in the field or surviving data from a particular period of history? The objective of a research paper focused on a body of scholarship is to find the source(s) of the debates among the scholars. The controversy might have arisen from differences in the questions that the scholars asked, or in differing views about how the evidence should have been collected, or in differing assessments of the reliability of the evidence.

The most general question about a scholarly debate is, "Why do scholars differ on this matter?" Just answering that question might be the basis of a paper, but in many cases you will have to find the specific issue on which they differ and formulate a question about it, such as, "Why do some scholars regard the data on race in the U.S. Census to be seriously flawed?" What makes this kind of paper a research paper is that it requires you to find the scholarship on the subject and then assess it. You have to formulate a question and a thesis about the scholarly treatment of the subject and construct an argument to support that thesis. If all you do is write a report on the scholarly literature you found, you will not have completed the assignment.

Finding Sources

How do you find primary and secondary sources? If you found your topic by reading, you will also have found some leads to further reading. The footnotes and bibliographies of the authors you have read will have given you a start. The Internet can also help, and you may already be in the habit of getting on the Internet to find what you need. You type a search term into a search engine and then sift through the hundreds or thousands of results. Some will be relevant, most will not. If the search term was reasonably specific, the items that come up at the top of the list are likely to be the most relevant to your interests. By defining your search terms, you impose order on what is actually a chaotic environment, and you increase the likelihood that you will find relevant information quickly. However, while the Internet's content is vast, in many fields of knowledge it is not even close to comprehensive and useful. The Internet is like a flea market. There are valuable things there, but you have to know how to judge value before you "buy." (There will be more on the reliability of Internet sources in the next section of this chapter.)

Caveats about relying on the Internet also apply to using documentaries, such as those broadcast on the History Channel, the Discovery Channel, and the National Geographic Channel. Some documentaries have valuable material in them, especially original footage of events that you may be interested in, but on the whole such documentaries are not very useful. They are not works of scholarship. They do not ordinarily reveal their sources or give any indication about how the filmmaker put the story together. The critical questions about the size and condition of the archive used are either not asked or not adequately answered as part of the film. The filmmaker rarely discusses other views of the subject or how he or she selected material to be included. In a few cases, professional journals publish scholarly assessments of documentary films, and such reviews can make the films quite useful,[1] but in general it is wise to avoid such sources.

Academic libraries are the best places to start. They contain materials chosen by specialists to represent the best information on a wide range of subjects, including nearly all of the kinds of subjects one deals with in research papers. Libraries purchase only a small percentage of what is published each year, but they typically acquire the kind of works most useful to faculty and students. Librarians purchase materials from publishers or sources that have established and respected processes for screening what they publish. They consult with faculty members about books and journals in their fields. Today, librarians also add websites to the library collection by creating links between their library web pages and the sites of organizations—such as scholarly associations or government agencies—that screen the content of their sites in a way similar to the way good publishers screen manuscripts.

Librarians have also organized the collections by author, title, and subject, so that a user can find materials by searching the catalog (now an electronic catalog in almost every large library) in a variety of ways. The subject catalog is a boon to anyone beginning a research project; in the course of more than a century of cataloging, librarians have developed an extensive, organized list of subjects. In the electronic catalog, you can also look for materials by keyword, as you do in Internet search engines. A keyword search will produce a list of materials in which the word appears, in the subject category, title, or, if the work has been digitized, in the text.

---

1. For example, *Perspectives,* the newsletter of the American Historical Association, occasionally reviews documentaries and films, and *The Chronicle of Higher Education* often does.

When you look at a book's catalog entry, you see a list of the subject areas under which the cataloguer classified it. Had you searched by one of those subjects, the book would have come up as one of your search results. Here is an example:

Author	<u>Woodward, C. Vann (Comer Vann) 1908-</u>
Title	**Origins of the new South, 1877-1913**
Published	[Baton Rouge] Louisiana State University Press, 1951
Description	xi, 542 p. illus. 24 cm
Series	<u>A History of the South, v. 9</u>
Note	"Critical essay on authorities": p. 482-515
Subject	Southern States -- History -- 1865-
	Southern States -- Social Conditions

(Library of Congress cataloguing data)

The cataloguer has classified this book under two subjects, each in the form of a composite string of headings and subheadings: "Southern States—History—1865–" and "Southern States—Social Conditions." In the first subject, "Southern States" is the main heading and appears alongside two subheadings: "History" and "1865–"; in this instance, "History—1865–" indicates that the history of the period after 1865 was a significant one for the Southern States. Had you searched the subject catalog under "Southern States" without including any subheading, the strings that include the subheadings "History—1865–" and "Social Conditions" would have appeared among your results, and *Origins of the New South, 1877–1913* would have been hyperlinked to both of the applicable strings. The catalog entry for every item in the library—book, video, or other medium—contains these kinds of subject identifiers.

Because you may begin your search without knowing the exact subject (or even the main heading) under which librarians have catalogued the kind of work you want, it is often a good idea to begin a search using the **keyword** command. Simply type in a term under which you think it might be promising to search and hit "search." A **simple keyword search** may yield results that are both relevant and sufficiently well defined to be of use to you; it may moreover help you discover a catalog entry for a book that proves of interest to you, one that reveals the exact subject entries under which books of the kind you want have been catalogued, which can in turn lead you to other titles of interest.

If the results generated by a simple keyword search prove unsatisfactory, you can often perform an **advanced keyword search** that generates results using Boolean operators; such a search can generate results that indicate: the conjunction of two or more keywords (that is, results that include this term **and** that term); the disjunction of two or more keywords (results that include this term **or** that term); or the exclusion of one keyword from another (results that include this term **when not associated with** that term). You come up with keywords and select the operators; the engine does the sifting.

Keyword searches turn up sources that contain both primary evidence and scholarly works. The keyword "Southern States" will produce a list that includes collections of data (primary sources) about the American south—data on population, the economy, public health, agricultural production, and so forth, as well as works written long ago, such as Arthur Fremantle's report on a three-month trip he took in the South during 1863 and scholarly works (secondary sources) like C. Vann Woodward's book on the origins of the new South. (Note that Fremantle's work is a report from direct observation and should be treated as primary evidence for a study of the South during the Civil War.)

Searches in library catalogs yield lists of books. They do not find articles published in scholarly journals or databases maintained by government agencies or scholarly institutes and databanks. There are many ways to find sources of those kinds. JStor is an online collection of scholarly journals that have been digitized. The collection contains journals in most disciplines of the humanities and social sciences and has volumes up to three years before the current issue. (For the most recent issues, you have to go to the library for the print copies.) You can get access to JStor through the web page of nearly all academic libraries, which routinely subscribe to the collection. You will also find guides to scholarly articles in such databases as the Social Science Citation Index, Sociological Abstracts, and the Annual Bibliography of English Language and Literature (ABELL), which list both primary and secondary materials. There are similar guides to sources in nearly every academic discipline, and most academic libraries list them under "Databases" or some such title on the homepage of their catalogs.

You may start by looking in that list, but you will be wise also to ask a reference librarian for help. Reference librarians are the scholar's friends. They know more about the resources of the library and the Internet than anyone else, and they are there to help you. Today, reference librarians are linked together in a large network, so if the local librarians cannot answer a question, they can send out a call for help to colleagues at libraries all over the country and beyond.

As with the search engines used to find things on the Internet, library catalog search engines list the search results in order of relevancy, as judged by the built-in rules that govern the engine's operation. In most cases, the books or articles that contain your search phrase in the title or those listed in a category from the subject catalog will be listed first, followed by works in which the phrase occurs many times in the text, and then by those in which it occurs only a few times, and so on. Before you start running around the stacks to retrieve material, look over the whole list, but expect to find the most relevant materials for your subject at the top of the list.

Evaluating the Credibility of Sources

When you walk into a campus library or access its electronic catalog, you make certain assumptions about what you will find there. You assume that people who know how to judge the credibility of sources, who know good scholarship from bad, and who choose the good and reject the bad selected the materials in the collection. You can use the materials you find in the library of a good academic institution with a lot of confidence that your instructor and others will regard the sources as serious works of scholarship and as reliable databases. However, serious works of scholarship can be seriously flawed. Scholars sometimes have biases and use evidence to reach predetermined conclusions rather than drawing their conclusions from disinterested analyses of the evidence. The conclusions drawn from work that was once regarded as sound may have been altered or overturned by further discoveries. As noted earlier, it is always smart to read reviews of scholarly books or to find articles that respond to or build on earlier works and, therefore, at least implicitly review the quality of the earlier studies. Scholarly reviews provide critical appraisals of books. The reviewers give you an idea about what the book covers, and then tell you how the book relates to earlier scholarship on the subject, and finally appraise the quality of the author's argument and use of the primary evidence.

Of course, selective and reliable as it is, the campus library is no longer the only or even the principal source of information for a research project. Many of you do most of your research on the Internet, where the credibility of sources is very uncertain. If you must be cautious when assessing books in the library, you have to be much more cautious when dealing with Internet resources.

The Internet is a great city with millions of sites in it, and more sites are being added every day. However, when you arrive at most sites you cannot assume that you will find credible information there. You need to pay attention to the authority of each site—who sponsors it, how often it is updated, and so on. The addresses of some sites give you a clue to their credibility. Sites sponsored by universities or their libraries (which are in the *.edu* domain), by government institutes or agencies (*.gov*), and by well-known scientific societies (such as the American Psychological Association or the American Political Science Association, which are usually in the *.org* domain) can be taken to be credible with the same confidence—and the same caveats— as the works found in an academic library. You are reasonably safe if you stick with such sites, though the *.org* domain contains a lot of sites to be wary of. The *.org* URL extension signifies that a site belongs to a nonprofit organization; it is not an indication that an agency has accredited the organization or the site. If you want to use other sites but do not know whether they are reliable, ask a reference librarian. They know a lot about the Internet. In addition, when you open a site, ask some basic questions:

- Does the site tell you who created it and who sponsors it? What can you find out about these people or institutions? Do they have an interest or agenda of some kind that might not be suggested by their name?

- Does the site tell you how its information was collected? For example, the Constitution Society has a website that contains documents and writings pertinent to the history of constitutions, especially the U.S. Constitution. The site gives you the provenance of each document, so you know how they got it and what it represents.[2]

- How is the information on the site managed? Is it kept up to date? If it offers a database that continually changes, how can you cite it so that the reader of your paper can find the particular data you used?

One thing these caveats make clear is that assessing the quality of evidence requires that you assess the quality of the sources that contain or provide it. Remember: Research requires you to pay attention to the credibility of sources.

As you read works on your topic, you will begin to go beyond just checking the identities of the creators of databases and the purveyors of information. You will develop a capacity to judge the quality of primary sources and scholarship. By reading critically, you will sift the information and opinions on your topic and begin to form your own opinion about which primary sources are most credible and which secondary authors most persuasive. Judgment of the credibility of sources proceeds from the question, "Should I read this?" to "Do I think this source is reliable or relevant?" and "Do I agree with this author's selection and interpretation of the primary evidence?" The characteristics of critical reading constitute the topic of Chapter 2.

---

2. If the site includes sources originally published in foreign languages, it may have digitized old translations because of copyright restrictions. You can get an idea of what an author was saying and then, if you wish to cite the work, search for, and compare it to, a more recent and authoritative translation in the library.

Chapter 2

Reading and Taking Notes

Once you have collected sources for your research project, you will have to read through all of them, looking for evidence that might support your argument and guidance from scholars on how to understand and interpret the evidence. To do so effectively, you will have to read the sources critically.

The key to reading critically lies not so much in learning specific techniques (though some practices are helpful) as it does in reading—and often rereading—with confidence in your ability to understand and respond to what you read. The critical reader is not passive; she takes a skeptical attitude. Her attitude is, "Show me"—even if she is not from Missouri.

The Tasks of Reading Critically

Once you begin reading confidently, certain techniques and practices can help you hold your own in the arena in which scholars are attempting to persuade you of their views. To engage a text actively you need to start with questions already in mind, including the following:

For primary sources such as results of surveys, census data, government records, contemporaneous accounts of events, etc.:

What inferences does the evidence, or data, support? What inferences does it fail to support? How was the evidence produced? How complete is the evidence a scholar has or that you yourself have? Sometimes you only have a small part of an archive that was quite large or a few samples of an artist's work. The question in both cases is, "How representative of the whole body of material is the part you have?" If the evidence comes from a survey, how was the survey conducted, was the sample adequate for drawing conclusions, and what questions did the surveyors ask? For example, when dealing with economic data about production in an industry, ask who collected the data, how it was collected, and for what purpose. When dealing with census data, ask whether the census-takers missed households, and how and why questions were phrased as they were.

For primary sources such as works of literature and art:

How was the work produced? Are there larger (artistic, historical, political, ideological, religious, etc.) contexts in which the work can be productively examined? In what ways does the work fit or not fit into such a context? How is the work similar to or dissimilar from other works of its genre? What does the work mean? What is the style of the work? How is its style related to its meaning? For what audience is the work intended? What is the artist's point of view? With what cultural biases is the author or artist imbued, and which does he or she challenge explicitly or implicitly?

For primary sources such as classic works of philosophy, theory, or thought:

What question is the author trying to answer? What does the author claim or how does he answer the question? What arguments does the author use to support his claims? Are the arguments persuasive? What are the key terms of the argument, how does the author use them, and what do they mean? For what audience is the author writing? Are there larger (historical, political, ideological, religious, etc.) contexts in which the work can be productively examined? What cultural biases does the work support or challenge?

For secondary sources (principally works of scholarship):

What question is the author trying to answer? What kind of evidence did the author use and does he or she use it fairly? In what kinds of sources did the author find the evidence? What is the author's point of view? How does the author make his or her argument? Is it persuasive? Who is the author's audience? (For example, it matters whether an author thinks he or she is contributing to historical or sociological scholarship, because the aims of historical sociology are different from those of history.)

As you read the scholarly works you have collected, you will also want to look for differences of opinion about the topic. Do the authors agree about what question needs to be answered about the topic? Do they use the same kind of evidence? When you compare them, do the authors differ in the emphasis they place on one part of the evidence or another? If they come to different conclusions—that is, propose different theses—why? What arguments lead the various authors to different conclusions?

Some points above that pertain to the reading of nonliterary primary sources and scholarly secondary sources are expanded upon thematically below. In reading for research, the main tasks include:

- **Identifying main ideas:** Identifying an idea implies being able to distinguish it from other ideas with which it might be confused. Try to formulate an author's main ideas in your own words.

- **Analyzing arguments:** This task includes distinguishing claims from the arguments marshaled to support them as well as distinguishing interpretations of evidence from the evidence itself. Look for how the author constructs his or her arguments; scholarly works will provide you with examples of arguments that will help you construct your own. Assess the quality of the argument in each work you read: Does the author provide sufficient evidence to convince you of her thesis? Do her assertions follow logically from the evidence she provides? Does the author contradict herself explicitly or implicitly? Does the author consider, and then rebut, arguments arising from other points of view or interpretations of the evidence? (If not, consider counterarguments the author should have rebutted and that might provide you an opening.) Any problems or contradictions you find might alert you to larger problems with the author's research as well as provide you with leads to topics for your own research.

- **Identifying point of view:** Every scholar has a point of view. For each new text you read, ask yourself from what perspective(s) the author views the topic. Try to find out something about the author and publisher of the work. Do they have political or other biases that you should look out for as you read? Pay attention to the date of publication. Every field of scholarship has a history; the more you understand about that history and how your author fits into it, the better positioned you are to understand his perspective—which may help account for his claims. He or she may adhere to a particular tradition in the field, such as a way of reading texts or a preconception about what certain words, passages, or clauses in a text mean. You'll find that many authors who write about religious subjects—even historians—come to their subject with beliefs that determine how they interpret the sources. For example, you'll find that the treatment an author gives a subject is often subtly influenced by his or her political views. An author who believes that people ought to be able to rise above their circumstances to achieve success in society—a view usually associated with conservative politics in the United States—may interpret evidence about the bureaucracy's examination system in 11th-century China as showing that the sons of poor farmers could rise to the top of society and that Chinese society in that period was open to talent. An author who believes that most people are trapped by circumstances and need help to break out of those circumstances—a view usually associated with liberal politics in the United States—might interpret the same evidence from China as showing that poor boys only rarely escaped the bounds of their poverty to rise into the ranks of the elite. The same evidence may be interpreted in opposite ways because of the different points of view of the authors.

- **Identifying approach:** Literary scholars and art historians often take particular approaches—such as neohistoricist, feminist, or psychoanalytic—to the works they interpret. If you are writing a paper for a literature course and reading a scholarly work to see how it interprets a novel you are writing about, pay attention to the types, aims, and assumptions of the questions she asks—not just the textual interpretation that she puts forth. Note that authors and artists are not always the main interest of literary and art historical studies. A scholar may be more interested in how literature and art reveal social values, politics, or even economic relationships in the society within which the works were produced. The scholar's interests will influence her approach.

Social scientists also take distinctive approaches to interpreting data, but they usually interpret it in a more quantitative manner than do humanists; you need to know what kind of data a particular social scientist uses (be it historical data, data from surveys, data collected from observation of social interactions, etc.) and how it was produced. As in the humanities, the same data can bear a number of different interpretations. And the interpretations themselves can proceed from many different starting points. A social scientist can be informed by any number of schools of thought and interpretation (e.g., in economics: Keynesian theory, free market theory, etc.) as well as by a variety of approaches to or interests in particular subjects (in anthropology: legal anthropology, cultural anthropology, etc.; in political science: political institutions, voter behavior, etc.). Reading critically means seeking to understand how an author approaches his or her subject and what his or her interests and aims are.

- **Identifying underlying theories and models:** Scholarly approaches to questions and evidence are often influenced by a particular theory to which a scholar subscribes. In both the humanities and social sciences, try to identify a scholar's theoretical allegiances. In the social sciences—in psychology and economics in particular—a given theoretical approach may also involve the application of a formal model. In economics, for example, a scholar starts with a hypothesis and uses a particular theory or predictive model that guides the way she looks at data on how people, institutions, or economies have behaved in the past and can be predicted to behave in the future.

  Pay attention to the nature of the data used by a scholar and the theories or models on which a scholar's interpretation of the data rests. Such theories and models require scrutiny, and some may have been developed in settings other than the one in which the author you are reading has applied them, even if the settings have important differences: Pavlov's experiments involving the conditioning of reflexes in dogs led to models by which environmental factors were held to condition ostensibly nonreflexive behavior in humans; modernization theory, which economists and other social scientists developed to describe a way for underdeveloped countries to increase wealth and improve social conditions, has been used by historians in their studies of the development of nation-states. A critical reader looks for such underlying schemes, whose strengths and weaknesses—in themselves or in the manner in which they are applied—support or undermine the foundation on which a scholar's arguments rest.

- **Identifying patterns:** In historical, sociological, and anthropological research, look for the following: recurring phenomena (such as the boom/bust cycle in market economies or the way people answer survey questions on a given topic); characteristics common to peoples of different times, classes, or cultures (such as the treatment of minority or immigrant groups or the representation of certain themes in art); themes that recur in the work of a variety of scholars (such as Keynesian or anti-Keynesian views of economic development, as noted above). In literary research, note both recurrent themes—such as the desire for power, the interplay of passion and reason in relationships, and hypocrisy—and the language authors use to express or represent those themes.

    An author's choice of words and images is often a terrific place to look for patterns. Authors use language to represent and persuade as well as to convey. Metaphors, similes, metonymy (the use of the name of a characteristic part of a thing to represent the thing itself, such as "the crown" for "the king and his council"), and other figures of speech don't merely convey the information they ostensibly convey; they also show how an author wants an audience to respond to that information.

    Pay close attention to key terms and how they are used in different contexts. For instance, the historian J. H. Hexter provided a great example of the importance of linguistic usage when he showed that in *The Prince,* Machiavelli almost always put "the state" in the syntactical position of an object of a verb. For Machiavelli, the state is a thing to be seized, protected, built up, lost, and so forth. It is not itself an actor,

but something acted upon; princes are the actors. Hexter's
observation gave readers a new understanding of Machiavelli's
conception of statecraft.[3]

• **Identifying connections between text and context:**
Look for meaningful connections between the content of
a text and the context (e.g., historical, sociological, political,
ideological) in which it was written. How, if at all, did the
work affect such events or developments? How, if at all, was
it affected by them? For example, Thomas Hobbes wrote a
"scientific" treatise on the origins and nature of political communities during the time his contemporaries were founding
the Royal Society in London. Was there a connection? Did
the new movement in what was then called "natural philosophy" have an effect on Hobbes?

• **Paying attention to the treatment of a work by other
scholars:** When you first read it, you may take a book or
article seriously because an apparently credible author wrote
it, a good academic press or journal published it, and a good
research library collected it. Later, you may find that most
scholars writing on the topic regard the work as seriously
flawed. Be alert to the judgments that scholars make about
others' works and the reasons they give for their opinions.
Often authors put these judgments in footnotes; pay attention
to footnotes even if they appear at the back of the book. Endnotes are a mere typographical convention, not an indication
that the notes are less worthy of attention than notes set at the
bottom of a page.

• **Recording areas for further research:** If the topic of a
work is one that interests you and you want to follow up on
it, note those areas that the author does not cover or covers
inadequately, either because she has not persuaded you or because she has not addressed other arguments that might lead
to conclusions different from hers.

• **Following the trail of scholarship:** No search of the library catalog will identify everything you need or should read

---

3. J. H. Hexter, "Il Principe and lo stato," *Studies in the Renaissance* 4 (1957):
113–35.

for your project. As noted in Chapter 1, the scholars you read have done a great deal of work for you and recorded it in their footnotes and bibliographies. Take advantage of what they've done. You can follow a trail of scholarship from a recent work to earlier works and from works that are central to the topic you are currently reading about to works that touch on that subject tangentially but that may become important for you as you define your topic and shift your focus. You start your research by searching the catalog of your library and searching the Internet, but you pursue your research by following the trails blazed by earlier scholars. You want to cite the scholarship you read, because you have learned from it and because you get credit from your readers if you show that you considered the ways in which your work fits into the scholarship on your subject. (There will be more on acknowledging your sources later in this chapter and in Chapter 7.)

The Mechanics of Reading Critically

Note-Taking

By taking notes as you read you will keep up with what you are reading. When you take notes, you have to think about what the authors are saying and about your response to their work. Taking notes is a vehicle for your engagement with the texts. Here's some advice for going about it:

- **Avoid merely summarizing the content of the text. Instead, summarize the text's main ideas.** For an article, record the author's key argument and the main points of that argument. For a book, summarize the main idea of each chapter (it's useful to note the chapter titles) and how each of the chapters relates to the overall argument of the book. You should stop to summarize as you read. If you wait until you've finished the book, you will probably forget some of the points that struck you as you read. If you find that a source contains so many useful pieces of information or so many tantalizing ideas that you want to make notes on many pages, then it's better to photocopy and to annotate key pages. (There will be more on annotation later in this chapter.)

- **Note key people, events, terms, dates, and phenomena.**
  These will provide the factual or evidentiary basis for your research paper. As noted earlier, you will find much evidence cited in secondary studies, because the authors use evidence to support their arguments. When you use evidence that you learned about from scholarly works, make sure to cite both the original document or database (the primary source) and the secondary source from which you took it.

- **Record your responses to the text. When you do, recall the following questions:**

  Questions about the author:
  > What is the author's research question?
  > What is the author's answer to the question? (The answer is the author's thesis.)
  > How does the author argue that the thesis is right?
  > What evidence does the author provide to support the argument?
  > Who is the author's intended audience?
  > For what purpose was the text written?
  > How does the author shape the argument to persuade his or her audience and achieve his or her purpose?
  > How might the author's purpose have affected how he or she selected and used evidence?
  > Which alternative arguments does the author address and how does he or she rebut them?
  > How persuasive is the author's argument?

  Questions about the text:
  > What questions does the text raise and which ones does it answer?
  > Why is the text important to your research?
  > How does the material connect with what you already know or have already read? Does it support or contradict what you have learned so far? Does it raise new issues?
  > Which ideas do you find interesting—and *why* do they interest you?

Annotating

As noted, there are times when it is useful to annotate a photocopied text instead of, or in addition to, taking notes on it. *To annotate* is to make notes in the margins. Annotate in pencil or in light-colored ink that doesn't obscure the printed text. (Generally, as noted below, highlighting is a bad practice, but here is a place where you might use a highlighter.) Highlight or underline the sentence or term that a marginal note relates to.

Useful annotation techniques include:

- **Underlining, bracketing, or highlighting main claims,** and noting in the margin, for example, "th" for "theme" or "arg" for "argument."

- **Circling or highlighting "pivotal words":** Words such as "however," "but," "nevertheless," and so forth indicate that the argument has changed direction. Add a marginal note to the passage indicating a change of direction (e.g., use a "Δ"— for "delta," the conventional scientific symbol for change). **Important Note:** What an author believes almost always comes *after* a pivotal word: for example, "Other scholars assert *x*, **but** I argue *z*," or "Horton's case for *x* is quite interesting. **However**, the evidence shows . . ."

- **Circling or highlighting key terms** and bracketing the definition, if it's provided in the text. (If the definition is provided, you might note "df" for "definition" in the margin.) If the author has not provided the definition, write the definition in the margin. When you can't pin down what an author means by a term, you may be at a doorway to your own topic and question. A murky term begs explanation—which could be what you end up writing about.

- **Marking where key people or groups, events, or phenomena are first described.** Circle or highlight a few key words in the text, such as the name of a person, the term used to describe a group (clan, tribe, class, family, etc.), and the name and date of an event, so that you can easily find the information again, and write a short note in the margin explaining what the marked item is.

- **Periodically noting the main idea of a passage.** For
  longer texts, it is useful to write a short (ten words or fewer)
  marginal note every page or two that summarizes the content
  of the page(s) and keeps track of the argument.

If you are reading a source that has been digitized, you may want
to use annotation software that permits you to make notes on the
screen. Such programs might be an efficient way to record your
responses to a text, whether on a computer or an e-reader. If you
use such software for some of your notes, you should think about
how you will use the notes when you organize your material
before beginning to write. Having notes in two or three different
forms and media could make it difficult to put them in order.

The Problem with Highlighting

Highlighters are handy, especially when annotating, but use of
them tends to get out of hand. They make you think you are
reading critically when you are not. You are just marking up the
text. Using highlighters

- **reduces** the likelihood that you will interact critically with
  the text. Highlighting doesn't allow you to distinguish between a main idea and a detail. If all you do is highlight, then
  it will be difficult for you to identify the key ideas, evidence,
  and arguments of the text when you are reviewing what you
  have discovered through research.

- **defers** critical reading. When you highlight, what you are
  really doing is saying to yourself, "I don't know what this
  means, but it *looks* important," or "I'll read this over again
  more carefully later on," whereas to read critically is to engage
  the text as you read it.

- **increases** the possibility that you will use too many quotations in your paper. You may even end up writing a paper that
  is just a collection of quotations. A paper composed of a string
  of quotations is a very bad paper. You've presented the findings and ideas of others but not your own thinking. Doing
  research is a sustained act of criticism, of finding and assessing
  information and arguments as you develop your own ideas. To
  the extent that highlighting interferes with that intellectual
  process, it undermines your entire effort.

Recording Necessary Bibliographic Information

One of the biggest problems in doing research is keeping track of what you have read. Research requires a great deal of clerical work. Take the time to record the complete bibliographical information on every work you read.

There is nothing quite as frustrating as finding the key datum or the perfect quotation to clinch your argument in a note that does not give you precise information about where you found or read it. When that happens (and every scholar can recite a list of his or her own experiences with incomplete notes) you have to spend hours going through what you've already done in hopes of finding the source. In many cases, you will spend the hours, fail to find the source, and then have to forgo use of the material. In the worst case, you'll have to revise your argument, and perhaps your conclusion, because the piece of evidence you can't trace to its source is crucial to making your current argument work.

Keeping accurate records of what you read and attaching the bibliographic information to your notes and to pages photocopied from sources will not only save you time—and perhaps your argument—but also prevent you from committing plagiarism. When students are caught using the words of others without quotation marks or citation, or when they paraphrase the words or ideas of others without citation, they often say that they must have just copied text from their notes into their paper—no plagiarism intended. Unfortunately, that's no excuse. Plagiarism consists in using someone else's work without acknowledging it. It can be intentional or unintentional. The latter may be less culpable than the former, but both intentional and unintentional plagiarism will lead to charges being filed and to a penalty that might be severe. (There will be more on plagiarism in Chapter 7.) If you do not know the source of information in your notes, you can't use it.

Here is the sort of information you need to record for everything you read:

- For books, the information includes the author(s), complete title, place of publication, name of publisher, and date of publication.

- For articles in journals or magazines, it includes author(s), complete title, name of the journal or magazine, volume number, issue number, date of the volume or issue, and inclusive page numbers. Specific volumes of journals and magazines are usually numbered by year—so, for example, the *American Political Science Review* for 2008 is volume number 102 (vol. 1 was published in 1906). The common practice is to refer to journals by volume, year, and page number—*American Political Science Review* (or *APSR*) 102 (2008), followed by the page numbers, but the style guide (such as the *Chicago Manual of Style* or the *Modern Language Association Handbook for Writers of Research Papers*) may specify a different practice. Always follow the style guide assigned by your instructor.

• For Internet resources, note the URL, the author or authority that produced the site, and whatever pathways a reader would need to find the material you are using. Remember that many websites are dynamic and constantly in flux, so you might need to note who or what organization maintains the site, how often it is updated, etc. If you are worried that the information you are taking from a site will have been altered, moved, or removed by the time your reader goes looking for it, then print it out, noting the date and the exact location at the time you used it. For a paper written for a course, being able to provide your teacher with a printout that has full information might save you from a lot of trouble.

In general, err on the side of completeness. The costs of sloppiness in recording bibliographic information include spending hours searching for the information while a footnote waits to be completed or having to rewrite an argument because you cannot find the source of information or of a quotation crucial to solidifying a part of your argument. For some, the cost has included accusations of plagiarism when, desperate to complete the assignment—as students facing a deadline often are—the writer just includes the material without proper citation. When you are doing research, you must keep the best records you have ever managed to keep.

Recording Your Notes

Presumably, you will keep records on the materials you find on a computer. You can record ideas in word processing files, in spreadsheets, or in databases, depending on the type of material you are dealing with. Word processors give you more room to write your own notes and comments than spreadsheets or databases, but the latter permit you to attach comments to specific bits of data. Word processors even allow you to create an electronic version of the old note card system, and you can buy 3 x 5 or 4 x 6-inch card stock to print out the e-cards. You need to think about how you want to keep your notes and records at the beginning of your project.

In general, you should keep the notes and records from each source in a separate file, named with the author or title of the source. In some cases, you may collect data of a similar type from several sources, and it makes sense to put all the records and notes in a single file of a spreadsheet or database. Just make sure that you mark the source of each record and have a file with the bibliographical information about every source you use. A common way to mark a record is with the name of the author, the date, and the page number—for example, Churchill (1948) 143 would indicate that the record comes from something by Churchill published in 1948 on page 143. Whatever system you choose to use, be careful to be consistent throughout your work. Otherwise, you are likely to make mistakes of citation when you finally write your paper.

During the early stages of working on a research paper, expect to read through a great deal of stuff, to take a lot of notes, and to make many photocopies and annotate copiously. You could also benefit from occasionally writing exploratory paragraphs that lay out ideas for the paper. In these paragraphs you can take stock of where you are and record ideas that you might forget later. It is only *after* you have accumulated a great deal of information that you can start to organize your work into a coherent topic that will produce a good paper. What you are aiming for is to formulate a research question, which will determine the direction of your research in the next stage of your work. Formulating a research question is the subject of Chapter 3.

Chapter 3

Formulating an Open-Ended Research Question

In many paper assignments, the professor asks you to write a paper with a thesis. (A thesis is a declarative statement that something is true.) Your job is to defend the truth of the statement by constructing an argument to support it. Examples of theses include the following: "The American criminal justice system is biased against certain social groups"; "Evangelical Protestants vote less conservatively than the press says they do"; "The financing of the railroads in the 19th century brought about the development of modern capitalism." In the course of your research, you have to formulate a thesis about your subject, but the typical assignment does not tell you how to do that. You do it by posing a question about your topic: **A paper that proposes a thesis starts with a question. Your thesis is the answer to the question.** Thus you reach a crucial stage in the work on your paper when you formulate a research question, or if the assignment gave or suggested one, when you have done enough work to understand the question in depth.

Before you can formulate your question, you have to bring some order to what you have been reading and thinking. If you have been reading critically, you will have a list of questions in your notes. Now you select (or, if necessary, synthesize) one narrow, open-ended question from all of the potential research questions you have accumulated. That question will provide the basis for your research paper and guide your research from that point on. Remember that you will be trying to answer this question and your argument must make a persuasive case that your answer is right or at least better than other possible answers. There will be more on arguments in Chapters 5 and 6, but first a discussion of questions.

Good Questions

You want an open-ended question: one that can be answered with justification, though not definitively. A question that you can answer by looking something up in a reference book is not a research question. You need a question that can be answered in more than one way, because you need to make an argument that your answer is a good one. A great deal of the scholarship found in libraries, the kind done by your professors, answers open-ended questions, which is why you will find many books and articles on some topics. For example: How do gender and religious beliefs intersect in voting patterns? The answer will depend on what evidence one looks at (from which voting districts, which segments of society, which economic class), on what issues were prominent during a certain election, on the way the candidates identified themselves to the electorate, on how one interprets the evidence, and on the statistical models one uses.

A research paper is not a report. In a report, you just summarize the information you've found and perhaps make some comments on the way scholars have gathered or treated that information. In a report, you merely show that you've read and understood a body of material. **Avoid writing a report.**

Even if your research paper assignment is to review the research on a particular topic—a task very different from that of writing a report—you will not have written a research paper unless you go beyond summarizing the scholarship you read. A good review of scholarship finds the question that the scholars are answering, even if none of them self-consciously set out to answer that question. The kinds of questions one answers in a review paper include the following: "No matter what purported or apparent questions the scholars ask and answer, what is the larger or actual question that they all are in fact answering?" "Why do the scholars who have written on a topic ask different questions (if they do)?" "Why do scholars writing on a topic use the evidence in different ways and thus come to different conclusions?" For example, if you are writing about the way scholars have treated the role of law (as opposed to such social systems as kinship) in tribal societies, you might propose that the general question that all of them are addressing is something like, "Can one apply Western (European and American) concepts of law to such societies?" Each of the scholars you read might be asking about the role of law in a particular society; you have stepped back and are asking a broader question about the whole enterprise of using concepts of law to understand the way such societies regulate behavior. By stepping back you will be on the way to producing a research paper based on your own question, not merely a report based on your reading. In the end you will have reached a higher intellectual level than could be reached in a report.

The answer to an open-ended question can be strong or weak, supported by a strong or a weak argument. A good thesis is one supported by a good argument. A good argument persuades because the evidence supports it.

Here are some examples of open-ended questions and the academic fields in which they would be posed:

- What effect does a flat tax have on an economy? (economics)

- Why do people continue to smoke even though they've been warned about the dangers cigarettes pose to their health? (neurophysiology, psychology, sociology)

- What was the primary cause of the American Civil War? (history)

- How did the use of camera obscura affect the development of painting in the late 19th century? (art history)

- How can James Joyce's short story "The Dead" be interpreted? (literature)

None of these questions can be answered definitively; each of them has several plausible answers that can be supported with evidence and argument. In other words, advancing and supporting an answer to any of the questions—to any open-ended question—necessarily means making an argument, which is your principal task when writing a research paper.

Basing your research project on an open-ended question thus provides two benefits, both of which involve elements of suspense and, often, of exhilaration. First, it gives you something interesting to figure out, so that your research becomes a process of discovery. Can you find evidence to support the answer you would like to give to the question? Second, it enables you to write a paper that advances a compelling argument. Can you convince your readers to accept your answer?

Research questions come in all sizes. Some good research questions need book-length answers based on years of research in out-of-the-way archives or months living in a community, doing surveys, studying government databases, or working in a laboratory. Others can be dealt with in short papers or articles. You have a few weeks to produce a ten-to-fifteen-page paper. You will need a question suitable to that task.

Why an Open-Ended Question That's Narrow?

Ten to fifteen pages, although it might seem endless to you, is really not very much space in which to make a compelling argument. You will need to narrow the scope of your topic and question in order to ensure that you can adequately explain your answer in the permissible number of pages. For example, you might be interested in how the rulers of the Roman Empire succeeded in establishing hegemony over conquered states. What, then, would be a sufficiently narrow research question for you to pursue in a ten- to fifteen-page research paper?

As an example, consider the problem of governing the vast empire that Rome had conquered by 100 CE. You might end up focusing on one province, such as Egypt, which was dominated by the Romans during the first century BCE and became a Roman province in 30 BCE, when Cleopatra VII committed suicide. Julius Caesar visited Egypt in 48 BCE; Marc Antony, Caesar's right-hand man, made Egypt the base of his power after Caesar's assassination in 44 BCE. Some questions you might entertain follow:

Much too broad:
How did Rome maintain control over its empire?

Still too broad:
How did Rome maintain control over Egypt?

Better:
How did Rome maintain control over Egypt in the first century BCE?

Better still:
How did Julius Caesar and Marc Antony control Cleopatra's governance of Egypt?

Formulating Your Question

Some of the questions you record during the process of reading critically (see Chapter 2) will lead to good research questions. Using the following criteria will help you decide which questions are most likely to be productive.

Classifying Questions by How, or Whether, They Can Be Answered

You can classify questions according to whether, how definitively, and with what evidence (if any) they can be answered. It helps to think of questions in terms of the following classes:

Class 1: Questions that can be answered with knowledge you
         have right now
Class 2: Questions that can be definitively answered with research
Class 3: Questions to which an answer can be proposed based
         on research but that cannot be answered definitively
Class 4: Questions that cannot be answered with research be-
         cause of a lack of evidence
Class 5: Questions that cannot be answered because they ask
         something that cannot be answered by citing evidence

You want to find a Class-3 question—an open-ended question that is answerable on the basis of available evidence—as the basis of your research paper.

The way you frame your question will have great consequences for the viability of your research project. Answering a Class-1 or Class-2 question (such as "How did women vote in the 2008 election?") will produce only a report, since you'll be able to find the answer to that question in post-election surveys.

A Class-4 question, such as "Did the majority of Roman citizens really believe that the emperor Augustus was a god?" cannot be answered because there are no surveys, diaries, or other evidence of what Romans thought about the matter. There is nothing wrong with the question as such—you could answer it if there were evidence to analyze and draw conclusions from— but in the absence of evidence you can only speculate about what the Romans might have thought.

A Class-5 question cannot be answered with research, because the answer to such a question rests not on observable, testable evidence but on beliefs. "Was the emperor Augustus a god?" is such a question. What evidence could you find to answer it?

If you want to produce a strong, interesting research paper, you must start with what at least appears to be a Class-3 question.

Types of Questions and Answers

Scholars distinguish between many types of questions, and a question may be of more than one type. It will help you a great deal to understand the type of question you are asking, because the type determines both the kind of evidence you have to find and the way you argue that your answer is the best one. A question of a given type calls for an answer of the same type. Identifying the type of question you are asking will also help you refine your question.

Perhaps the most basic distinction among questions of the kind suitable for research papers is that between **normative** and **descriptive** questions. A *normative* question asks what action or type of action should be taken, what state of affairs ought to exist, what values should be privileged over other values, and so forth. "How should the United States organize its health care system?" is a normative question. Do people have a right to health care? What is the community's obligation to provide health care in comparison to the responsibility of individuals to arrange and pay for their own care? While a normative question can require research—for example, to discover the current state of health care and the proposals to reform the system—the thrust of the question is evaluative or prescriptive. The answer to such a question engages issues of value and moral or aesthetic principle. The task set by the question is to formulate a position of one's own and defend it, or to support a position found in the literature on the subject and explain why it is the best position.

A *descriptive* question asks about past, present, or future states of affairs. In effect, it asks what is observably or predictably the case, not what should be or what ought to be the case.[4] "What do Americans think the health care system should be?" is a descriptive question. It asks for a description of Americans' opinions. Do they

---

4. The term "empirical" is also used to designate questions and claims on the "is" side of the "is/ought" divide.

believe that people have a right to health care? Do they think that the community should provide it? If they think the community should provide health care, what limits do they put on the community's obligation? The answers to the main and subordinate questions will be found in opinion surveys, political platforms, and other sources that provide evidence of what Americans think.

In some fields of the social sciences, particularly in sociology, the term "normative question" has a special meaning. In these fields, a normative question asks what the underlying and determinative values of a community or society are. Questions such as "How do Americans think about health care?" look like descriptive questions and are answered as if they are, using opinion surveys and the like. But they are considered normative by those sociologists who think that what happens in a society is determined by its underlying values. Norms drive action. Other sociologists reject this idea and think that what happens in a society—the way people think about issues or subgroups in the society among other things—cannot be traced to social values or norms. They focus their work on describing how opinions and attitudes are represented in the society and how they affect what happens in social action, such as the growth of grassroots movements or religious communities.

The distinction between **qualitative** and **quantitative** questions is also a basic one. This distinction affects the way a question is answered more than how it is phrased, and some questions can be answered in either way, or in a way that draws from both approaches, while other questions call unambiguously for one or the other approach.

A *qualitative* question or answer is one based on evidence of what people say or how they represent an idea. Thus, a qualitative answer to the question, "How do you define the American family?" will rest on what Americans say the definition is when surveyed or interviewed. The scholar might also cite the way movies and television shows portray families. A qualitative response to the question would produce one or more definitions of the family, all of them representing the response or responses of some group.

A *quantitative* question or answer is based on statistics—that is, on how many or what proportion of instances of something there are. A quantitative answer to the same question about the American family will take into account data about actual domestic arrangements, such as from census data, which might lead a scholar to the conclusion that what people say the family is has little in common with what one finds when looking at facts on the ground. A quantitative study might find that a significant proportion of actual domestic arrangements involve only one parent, while another involves parents who have been married before and have brought children into their marriage. Other arrangements might have two parents who are unmarried and many include no children. A scholar taking a quantitative approach to defining the family will discard the ideal or even seemingly realistic definitions that people formulate from their own experience and ideas and rest her answer on quantitative data drawn as directly as possible from the relationships themselves.

One way to characterize the difference between quantitative and qualitative approaches is to say that quantitative research describes what people actually did or do and qualitative research describes what they say they did or do. Which approach provides more useful knowledge? That's a question endlessly debated in many disciplines.

In sociology, those who regard the calculus of data to be the foundation of knowledge apply statistics and other mathematical techniques to large data sets, such as census records and surveys, to answer questions about how society works. Those who think that attitudes, ways of reasoning, and other components of human behavior tell us more than numbers can about social phenomena base their work on interviews and surveys that aim to reveal such qualitative information about individuals and groups. We've seen how these two approaches differ in the discussion of the question about the definition of the American family.

In political science, a quantitative study of voting uses data of various types, such as exit polls, party affiliation, and income, to answer questions about what happened in an election and perhaps to predict what will happen in future ones. A qualitative study of voting relies on interviews and other ways of finding out what people think, and it looks at issues as defined by news organizations, party platforms, and polls to answer such questions.

As noted, some questions—such as whether Americans support gay marriage—can be answered either quantitatively or qualitatively; often, however, one formulates a question in a way that calls for one or the other approach. If you believe that the best way to understand your subject is by counting, then you should formulate your question so that it can be answered by quantitative analysis. If you believe that the most important aspects of your subject are qualitative, then you should formulate your question accordingly. A quantitative question about voting patterns might be, "What was the effect of income on how people voted in 2006 on a school bond in Cleveland?" A qualitative question on the same subject might be, "What was the effect of people's views about education on the way they voted on the bond?"

Questions can also be categorized in several other ways. As seen in our discussion of approaches to a question about the nature of the American family, one question type is that of **definition**. What does such a question seek to accomplish? In most research in the social sciences and humanities, questions of definition don't aim to clarify some unchanging "real essence" of an institution, or some "real meaning" of a concept, but rather to recognize the institution or concept in question as socially constructed and to seek definitions that while not arbitrary are useful (rather than "true"), historically informed, and admittedly provisional. Consider again the question "What is the American family?" If you pose this question, you won't be after some timeless answer. Rather, you might be after one that usefully and clearly reflects a widely held though largely ignored understanding of the institution, or after a new definition that can be shown to have some clear advantage over a widely held one. In either case, you might begin by stipulating a definition (in this case, a provisional, working definition) in a study that concludes— on the basis of analyzing quantitative data, qualitative data, or both—by revising and refining that definition. Alternatively, you might not stipulate a definition at all but rely on subjects to tell you, through questionnaires or interviews, how they understand the American family and then analyze the results.

Questions can also concern what we normally call **facts**. The concept of "fact" is a tricky one, because while we generally use the term to denote a bit of information that is incontrovertible, such as a person's date and place of birth when there is a valid birth certificate that specifies both, we also use the term loosely to denote bits of information that appear to be true on the basis of a preponderance of the evidence. A great deal of scholarship deals with questions of fact—that is, the scholar is trying to show that something happened at a particular time and place or that some institution, such as the family, U.S. Congress, or the American stock market, has certain characteristics. Answers to "fact" questions seek to establish the truth of a claim. Such efforts consist of arguments that certain evidence makes it extremely likely that a claim is true; you are arguing that the claim is a fact. One example of this sort of question is, "Did Shakespeare write the plays attributed to him?" There is no incontrovertible evidence that William Shakespeare did in fact write the plays—no manuscripts of the plays in his handwriting or with his signature on them, no extant comments by a contemporary linking him with particular plays, no records of the Globe Theater showing that he wrote any of the plays presented there, and so forth. The thesis that Shakespeare wrote the plays is thus not a fact but a claim, which has to be supported with arguments based on evidence. The aim of the scholar is to persuade us that her claim is true—that is, that we should accept it as a fact.

Questions can be about **causes** (and effects) as well as **purposes.** "What were the main causes of the Great Depression of the 1930s?" "What is causing the apparent shift of Americans' attitudes toward same-sex marriages?" Note that in both of these questions, the first term—the Great Depression and the shift in attitudes—has to be taken as a fact; there can be no question about whether there was a depression in the 1930s or whether there has been a shift of attitudes about same-sex marriage. If a question about the first term exists—for example, whether a shift of attitude has been taking place—then you will probably end up writing about that question, which is one of fact, not cause. You can take the historical reality of the phenomenon known as the Great Depression for granted because both you and your readers know that it was and remains extremely well documented;[5] you may need to cite evidence for a shift of attitudes toward

---

5. A separate issue is the categorization or periodization of social and historical phenomena and the labels by which such phenomena are referred to. Were the "L.A. riots" of 1992 riots or rebellions? Was "the Renaissance" real? See W. K. Ferguson, *The Renaissance in Historical Thought* (Boston: Houghton Mifflin, 1948), and H. Brown, "The Renaissance and Historians of Science," *Studies in the Renaissance* 7 (1960): 27–42.

marriage—for example by noting that all the polls done in the last five years show that it is happening—before launching an analysis of its causes. In either case, your answer needs to adduce evidence that shows why the change occurred.

A question about purpose is similar to one about cause—but trickier. When you ask about someone's purpose or intent in doing something—for example, "What was Madison's intent in framing the freedom of religion clause in the Bill of Rights as he did?"—you must support your answer with arguments based on historical evidence, as you would in answering a question about any historical cause; but, in addition, you should formulate your answer in terms of the risks and consequences foreseen and un-foreseen by the agent, as well as the interests served or thought to be served by the action taken. You are trying to look through the eyes of someone who could not know what you know about how things turned out—yet you cannot know all the reasons they had for doing what they did.

Answering a question about the cause of some event or about someone's purpose in doing something requires you to consider what constitutes a cause and an effect. We think of a cause as a reason why a given change takes place or a given state of affairs exists.[6] But when can you say that one event or change causes another? Sometimes, you find direct evidence that something happened because of an earlier event or change. Most of the time, however, you have to infer, under circumstances that leave a good bit of room for doubt, that x caused y.

Consider the question "Why do American Protestants fre-quently migrate from one denomination to another?"[7] If this were

---

6. An *account* of how or why a change takes place or why a given state of affairs exists is an *explanation,* which provides a reason. The argument of a research paper is often, in this sense, an explanation. But see Chapter 6 for a discussion of *explanation* in a different sense—the explanation of evidence.

7. Note that the question focuses on denominations, not congregations. A person might change congregations within a denomination, but this ques-tion deals with those cases in which people change denominations when they change congregations. Finding that such changes are frequent, one might infer that for Protestants it is the nature of the congregation, not of the denomination, that induces them to join. For more on this sample question and approaches to it, see Chapter 5.

your question, you would try to find data from surveys and other sources that allow you to relate the act of changing denominations to other events in the lives of the people who made the move. You might find that there is a spike in the number of migrations from one denomination to another when people marry. That finding is evidence that changes of marital status affect the choice of denomination, but the correlation of the two events might just be coincidence. (Note that establishing a correlation between two things is relevant to, but insufficient for, establishing that one thing caused the other—let alone establishing which caused which.) To strengthen an argument that getting married often causes one of the new spouses or the couple to change denominations, you need either some testimony, perhaps from a survey that asked people why they changed denominations, or some other correlations that confirm the connection between marital status and choice of denomination. If, for example, you found that there is also a spike in the incidence of denominational migration when couples get divorced, you would be in a better position to argue that changes in marital status cause changes in denominational membership.

Questions can also be about **policy**, both how policies put in place in the past worked out and how or whether new ones will work. For example, "Did the social welfare reforms passed during the Clinton administration reduce poverty and social dependence?" or "Will the regulation of financial institutions to limit the kinds of transactions they may carry out reduce the incidence or severity of future market crashes?" These questions call for different kinds of analysis and argument. The first one, a question of both fact and causality (though framed in terms of effect rather than cause), requires you to study the evidence collected by government and private agencies that track what happened to welfare recipients after the reforms. The argument in support of one answer or another consists in the interpretation, or explanation, of the data. The second question, similar to a question about purpose in that it forces you to imagine a future and its contingencies, requires you to look at how the policy will work in light of the efforts of financial institutions to earn profits in any way they can. You might construct a model to test the policy's operation and then predict, on the basis of the evidence produced by the model, whether it will reduce the frequency or severity of future financial meltdowns.

Just as you can answer some questions both by quantitative and qualitative approaches, you can also answer questions from more than one **perspective.** For example, if you are asking, "Why did Europeans become dominant in the world in the early 19th century?" you might frame an answer by comparing economic, technological, or cultural development in Europe and other major civilizations of the period. Each of these approaches to the question requires different kinds of theoretical models, evidence, and bodies of scholarship. Likewise, if your topic has to do with the nature of the American family, you might ask, "What effect has technological development had on the family?" or "What effect has the feminist movement had on the family?" or "How do religious beliefs affect relationships within a family?"

So, take a critical approach to your research question—just as you do to the books and articles you read and to the data you study. Paying attention to question types and to the approach you want to take gives you a clear sense of what sort of evidence and arguments you need to answer your question. When you know what type of question you are asking and what approach you will take, you know how to work with what you have already found in your research and where to look for additional evidence. You also have a good idea of what sort of argument you will have to make.

Keeping Track of Questions, Ideas, and Evidence

One good way to get to a research question that will serve your needs is to start to identify questions early in your research process. Write down each research question that occurs to you as you get into the research process. Keep a separate file for each one, and record or photocopy all of the evidence you find that might help you to answer the question, along with your annotations, notes, and comments. By the time you get to the stage where you have to make a choice, you'll have a lot of possibilities to choose from.

Chapter 4

Working toward an Answer to Your Research Question: Focusing Your Reading, Considering Arguments, and Refining Your Question

Once you have a good question, you will be able to focus your reading by looking for evidence in primary sources and interpretations of the evidence in secondary sources that will help you answer your question. You will also be able to review what you read earlier with your question in mind. You will be amazed how much new information and how many new ideas you can see in previously read texts once you have the focus that a research question provides.

As you return to reading, you will probably have some idea about how you want to answer the question—that is, what your thesis will be. This tentative thesis, too, will help you choose what to read. However, keep an open mind. You may discover that your first impressions about how the project will turn out are wrong and that you arrive at a different conclusion after doing your research.

Exploring Arguments and Counterarguments

As you begin to read again ask yourself what you have to show to be true to make a good argument in support of your tentative answer to the question. Most arguments consist of a series of claims that you must show to be true or at least more than merely plausible. The argument you make to support each claim consists of citations of evidence and the reasoning that justifies the citations.

Here is an example. If your question is, "What was the original purpose of the Parliament in England?" you will start with a claim about when the institution was created, citing evidence that shows when that happened and referring to the work of scholars who have written about it. Then you must make a claim you think you can defend about what the evidence produced by, about, and before the early Parliaments shows about its purposes or function. You should record as many plausible claims as you can. One claim could be that the kings created Parliament as a political body to help them govern. Another claim could be that kings created Parliament as a concession to economically powerful English counties and towns whose populations wanted to be heard on national issues. Yet another claim might be that whatever purposes the kings had in mind, the principal business of the early Parliaments was the hearing of petitions and law cases brought to the meetings by members and others. So, the Parliaments were not so much political bodies as courts, the highest in the land because the king presided in the presence of the representatives of the whole kingdom. As you work toward your answer to your question, you need to argue for or against these claims or hypotheses, presenting the evidence that supports or contradicts each of them. You will build the argument for your thesis from claims and the demonstrations of their truth or likelihood. You should structure your argument—that is, arrange your individual claims—to make it flow logically toward the conclusion you have drawn from your research.

This example shows that a good argument is not necessarily completely positive. Sometimes, you build an argument only of claims that you think the evidence and sound reasoning support, but that is not common. Most often, a good argument deals with claims—representing possible answers to your question or the subquestions it raises—that you want to reject as well as those you think are supportable. The rejected claims or hypotheses are counterarguments, and they strengthen your main argument by showing that you have considered other possible answers and by dealing with evidence that you have decided is not significant but that a reader might point to if you didn't. Imagine your reader saying, "Oh really? What about these documents that show that . . ." If you have considered counterarguments, you have shown or at least argued that those documents don't undermine your answer to the question. The use of counterarguments is part of what scholars call the rhetoric of persuasion, and it is good to keep in mind that your aim in making an argument is to persuade your reader that you are right.

Your question guides you in figuring out what you need to know to answer it. What evidence and background material will you need to cover? What kind of claims will you have to make or deal with? What points will you need to make?

If, for example, you wanted to address a question about how the French are dealing with their immigrant populations, you would need to consider:

- The number and origins of the immigrants in a given period.

- The patterns of settlement—where do the immigrant populations live?

- The kinds of evidence available: opinion surveys, legislation, economic data about the role of immigrants in the economy and how they are doing relative to native French people, political campaigns and party platforms, newspaper and television news portrayals of immigrants, portrayals (including self-portrayals) in the arts, particularly movies, literature, and popular music. All of these kinds of evidence are relevant.

- What scholars—particularly sociologists and political scientists—have written about the response of the French to resident immigrants.

Reflecting on Your Research Question as You Proceed

As you continue reading, you may revise your research question several times. You may find that you cannot gather what you think is the right kind of background information. You may find that you cannot give a plausible explanation, with supporting evidence, of one of the points you thought you would have to make to answer the question as you formulated it. You may recognize that your question is too big; you would need too much time and too many pages to answer it. The focused reading that you do at this stage of your work will take you into the heart of the argument that will support a satisfactory answer to your question. Whenever you feel that you have a mass of undigested material—information that you know is relevant to your topic but that you do not feel in control of—stop and reassess.

At these stopping points, you should try to organize your notes and rough out some paragraphs or pages setting down your view of what it all means. Writing forces you to put your ideas in order and articulate them—at least to yourself. Writing is a way to help you think, and thinking is what you need to do to write a good paper. Seeing your ideas on paper will help you assess them. Then you should look at your research question again. How do the materials you've collected and the thoughts you've had help you answer the question? Do you have to revise the question? You can only answer a question if you find relevant information. You know that you have relevant information if you can use it to argue that an answer to the question is likely if not compelling.

You also need enough information. It will do you no good if you find material to answer one part of the question but not another. Thus, if you were working on the response of the French to immigrants, you might have found evidence of what politicians said in recent campaigns but no opinion surveys that would tell you how people outside the political arena viewed immigrants. In that case, you might have to revise your question to focus on the way the presence of significant immigrant populations affects French politics. Stopping to order and reflect on what you've found will speed your research and improve it. You will not get off course, and you will not spend time reading texts that do not serve your purpose.

Chapter 5

Answering Your Question and Constructing Your Argument

Give yourself time to develop your paper. Do not do research up to a couple of days before you have to turn it in. It is better to start transforming your notes and ideas into a coherent draft early rather than late. You can accomplish this task by working through the following steps.

Sort Notes and Texts

If you have been taking your notes on paper, gather all of the material you have generated in the course of your research: notes, copies of pages from primary and secondary sources, and pictures. Sort the material into piles representing different aspects of your topic. Each batch of materials might include notes on the evidence from primary sources and on scholarly opinions from secondary sources, annotated copies of pages you judged significant when you read them, and notes recording your own thoughts as you did your reading. If you have kept notes on the computer, sort them into categories and make an outline that puts the categories in an order. If you have notes on your computer and photocopied pages from sources, it might be best to print out the computer materials and organize everything in hard copy.

Sorting your research materials accomplishes a number of goals. First, it allows you to review all of the information you have gathered, alerting you to any gaps in your research and reminding you of some things you might have forgotten. Second, it reveals the way you now think you will argue the case that your thesis is sound. Third, it constitutes a first step in putting together a rough draft. The order into which you organize your piles of information will become the order in which you present that information in your draft.

Write a Working Thesis

You will probably already have formulated a thesis when you started the research on your question; if not, you will most likely find that it comes to you as you organize your notes. Write down your working thesis, stating it in a few declarative sentences. For example, here is a plausible working thesis that responds to the question of how resident immigrants affect French politics (the revised and narrowed question that resulted from your research):

> The presence of large numbers of immigrants in France has made immigration legislation and the rights of immigrants the second most important issue, after the state of the economy, in the platforms of French political parties and in their campaigns.

Note the coherence of this thesis. Regardless of whether it is true or false, regardless of whether your evidence and reasoning will support it, the proposition hangs together and is internally consistent. It does not contradict itself. **The first job of a thesis is to be coherent.** It cannot rise to the challenge of serving as an answer to your research question if it does not meet this minimal requirement.

Note the specificity of this thesis; it goes beyond a broad response—"Immigration and immigrants have become major political issues." It specifies the importance of the issue relative to other political concerns and points to party platforms and campaign rhetoric as supporting evidence. The more specific you can make your working thesis, the easier it will be to write your rough draft, and the more focused and coherent that draft will be.

The statement of the thesis points toward your main arguments, which will be built on evidence from party documents and analysis of campaign speeches and ads. You will have to rank the political issues raised in recent campaigns and argue that the evidence shows immigration to be the second most important one to politicians and voters. You might argue from the way elections turned out that the politicians did or did not have their fingers on the pulse of the people. You might analyze legislative activity and news coverage of it to reveal the relative importance of immigration issues beyond election campaigns.

This statement is a working, or provisional, thesis: one that you might change as you think through your research material during the course of writing your draft. Use your working thesis as a guide, but don't be afraid to change it if further reflection convinces you that you've found a better answer to your question.

Types of Arguments

Once you've formulated a working thesis you can refine the organization of the material you've collected. As you put your information in order you will create the outline of your paper: the train of information and explanation that leads readers from your research question through the main points of your argument to your conclusion or answer to the question.

You need a general understanding of arguments in order to build a good argument.[8] The most basic distinction among arguments is that between **deductive** and **inductive**. In a valid *deductive* argument—a form of argument of which there are many kinds—the conclusion follows necessarily from the premises. Here's a valid deductive argument of the most familiar kind:

All textbooks are dull. (premise)

Chodorow's *Europe in the Middle Ages* is a textbook. (premise)

Therefore, Chodorow's *Europe in the Middle Ages* is dull. (conclusion)

If the premises in a valid deductive argument are true, the conclusion cannot help but be true. Making such an argument requires logical reasoning, but it does not require research. Some readers of Chodorow's textbook, who would be engaged in a "research" enterprise, might conclude that it is not dull. Those doing research use inductive arguments.

An *inductive* argument begins with observations about the world and then draws conclusions from those observations. Obviously, such an argument does not just start by looking at the world. You have to focus your observations on some aspect of the world, which implies that you have some question or idea in mind. In its

---

8. For a more complete introduction to the nature of arguments, see A. Weston, *A Rulebook for Arguments*, 4th ed. (Indianapolis: Hackett Publishing Company, 2008).

classical form, an inductive argument starts with a hypothesis. For example, "In states that have public universities that play Division I football, the incumbent governor loses the election when the team has a losing record during the fall before the vote" (hypothesis, which could also be stated as a question). To test this proposition, you would look at the electoral results and win-loss records of Division I public university teams, collect the data over several election cycles, and draw your conclusion, which would be an affirmation or denial of the proposition. There are many subtypes of the inductive argument that your question might require.

Arguments from examples may lead to generalizations: "Conceptual art arose from the implication in Abstract Expressionism that art need not be a representation of reality but rather could express an idea about form, line, and color" (thesis). The argument in support of this thesis might cite writings of Abstract Expressionists, pop artists, and critics as well as specific artworks that, one could say, exemplify the move toward conceptual art.

Arguments from analogy draw a conclusion from a supposed likeness of two things in a given respect—such as events, organizations, or social or cultural values. Consider the following analogical thesis: "The social function of extensive libraries in the homes of college professors is analogous to that of large houses and expensive cars in suburban communities." A supporting argument would require a demonstration that suburbanites' houses and cars and professors' personal libraries all function similarly as status symbols. Research would focus on studies of status and its symbols in these two social sectors.

Arguments of interpretation treat the evidence as a text, even if the evidence consists of artworks or data sets instead of actual texts. "When American women began to keep their own surnames after marriage, the old idea that marriage is a bridge between two families made a comeback" (thesis). The argument supporting this proposition must interpret statements indicating that marriage was once (when and where?) a deal between two families; that it became (when and where?) a relationship between two people that certainly involved two families but not as principal decision-makers or determiners of the marriage; and that people really do see the recent practice of women keeping their family names as reviving the old idea. In effect, you would be arguing that a woman who chooses to keep her family name in marriage asserts that she represents her birth family, as does her husband, in the new household. Arguments of interpretation are common in sociology, anthropology, political science, and history, but they are most often found in literary studies and art history, where the main goal is to interpret or reveal the meaning of texts and works of art. (For more on interpretation see Chapter 6.)

The Organization of Arguments

The two basic ways to organize arguments are **chronological** and **thematic.** Arguments in history papers often proceed in a chronological framework, because they are often about how the past affected the future. Arguments in most other fields tend to be thematic in organization, although papers focused on change—such as one in sociology or political science that considers the change in attitudes toward same-sex marriage—can be organized chronologically.

As an example of a thematically organized argument, consider a sociology paper based on the question discussed in Chapter 3, "Why do American Protestants frequently migrate from one denomination to another?" An outline helps make the argument of such a paper clear.

I. Your study of surveys in which church-going American Protestants were asked whether and when they changed churches might show that

   A. Such Protestants switch denominations regularly, but that

   B. There are significant increases in the numbers in certain circumstances, such as

      1. When people move from one community to another and

      2. At certain ages, say 28–30 and 42–45.

   C. Men change denominations more often than women.

   D. When Protestants switch denominations, they are unlikely to join a non-Protestant Christian denomination or a non-Christian denomination.

II. From analyzing the findings of I., you might infer that the changes associated with relocation indicate that

   A. The decision to change congregations and denominations is driven primarily by social rather than theological reasons; that

    B. When people move, they look for a congregation in which they feel socially comfortable; and that

    C. They do not choose a congregation because they agree with the particular doctrines of the denomination with which the congregation is affiliated.

III. From looking at other data, you might note that

    A. The ages 28–30 are when the number of people getting married jumps, and that

    B. The ages 42–45 are when the largest number of divorces occur.

IV. By looking at I.A., B., and C., and III.A. and B. together you might infer that

    A. Men join the congregations favored by their new wives, and that

    B. When divorce occurs men are more likely than women to join other congregations within the community.

Both IV.A. and B. support the idea that joining a church is a social, not a theological, process by helping to account for the otherwise mysterious increase in denominational change after moving house and at certain ages, as noted in I.B.1. and 2., and for the gender disparity noted in I.C. Thus you might answer your research question with the thesis, "While Protestants have beliefs and social identities that differentiate them from, for example, Catholics and Orthodox Christians and that tend to prevent them from becoming Catholic or Orthodox, Protestants tend to change denominations for social reasons."

    To support your thesis, you could argue that changes in marital status and relocation are the best predictors of a change in denominational affiliation. You could organize your argument— that is, discuss your findings as well as account for the inferences you draw from them[9]—in various ways, but you should do it in

---

9. Notice that you could have put your findings in a different light: Noting that when Protestants change congregations, they usually join congregations of other Protestant denominations rather than non-Protestant congregations or even non-Christian congregations could suggest that Protestants recognize and regard as important the theological differences between Protestantism and, for example, Catholicism or Orthodox

a way that makes the account you wish to give of your findings clear, straightforward, and concise.

A good way to approach the organization of a thematic argument is to think of it as a story, one in which your arrangement of the elements—or even the process by which you discovered the elements—forms a plot. (To present a thematic argument as a story of course smuggles it into a chronological frame, but the result is likely to be more interesting than an argument that is purely thematic.) Even though your reader will have read your thesis at the beginning of your paper—and thus knows from the outset the claim for which you are arguing—telling how you arrived at your thesis can make for a good story. How do you want to tell it? (Note that, in the example just presented, it wasn't until you looked at I.A., B., and C. in the light of III.A. and B. that you were able to account for I.B.2. and C.—a discovery with some narrative potential.) As you organize the argument, think about how you would order your points if you were telling a friend what you had found and concluded when you studied the surveys and other data.

The Structure of the Paper

Just as your argument should flow logically from point to point, so your paper as a whole should have a logical structure. There are various ways to work toward one, as we'll see in the rest of this chapter and in Chapter 8.

Some students like to write an outline of the paper before they start writing the paper itself, setting out the topics and putting them into a hierarchy of importance. The thesis holds the place of honor, followed by necessary background information, and then the main arguments supporting the thesis.

Using an example already discussed, here is a sketch of an outline for the entire paper:

Christianity, while regarding the doctrinal differences among Protestant denominations as relatively unimportant. This interpretation gives an important role to theology or belief as a determinant of denominational affiliation while taking into account the findings themselves. For this reason—that a debatable question is really debatable—it's not enough to discuss your findings; you must also argue for your interpretation of them. (More on the interpretation of evidence in Chapter 6.)

Thesis: The presence of large numbers of immigrants in France has made immigration legislation and the rights of immigrants the second most important issue, after the state of the economy, in French political campaigns.

I. The Research Question and Thesis
   A. The question
   B. The evidence on the subject
   C. Possible theses
   D. My thesis

II. Background Information
   A. Immigrant groups
      1. How are immigrants grouped?
      2. How many immigrants in each group?
   B. Geography of immigrant communities
   C. The economy of immigrant communities
      1. In what sectors of the economy do immigrants work?
      2. Levels of unemployment
   D. Immigrants and education
      1. Average educational level of immigrants
      2. Immigrants in higher education
      3. Immigrants in the professions
         a. Law
         b. Medicine
         c. Other professions
   E. Immigrants and crime

III. Political Parties and Immigrants: The Evidence
   A. When did immigrants become a political issue?
   B. Political platforms
      1. Union for a Popular Movement
      2. Socialists
      3. National Front
      4. Etc.
   C. Stump speeches
   D. Campaign ads

IV. How Important Are the Issues Concerning Immigrants in the Political Process?
   A. Place of immigrant issues in party platforms

B. Amount of space devoted to immigrant issues in party publications

C. Percentage of political ads devoted to immigrant issues by various parties

D. Importance of immigrant issues in campaign speeches, including time spent on the issue relative to other concerns

E. Polls showing importance of immigrant issues to members of various parties

F. Time devoted to immigrant issues by print and broadcast news organizations

V. Outcome of Elections: What Do They Show about the Importance of Immigrant Issues?

An outline should reveal a structure for your paper, and looking at it should enable you to reorganize ideas so that they flow easily from one to another. In this example, the first task, carried out in the first paragraph of the paper, is to explain the research question and the possible answers to it. After explaining the question, which includes showing why it is a question worth answering, you need to indicate the kind of evidence needed to answer it and that you have found that evidence. Finally, you should sketch possible answers to the question, state which answer is the one you will defend, and at least hint at why you think your answer is the best one. A paper is not a piece of mystery writing; you do not want to leave your reader guessing how it will come out until the last paragraph. Rather, you are saying to the reader, "This is what I think the answer to the question is. Let me show you that I'm right."

If you are going to write about political responses to immigrants, it seems obvious that you need to begin the paper with information about those groups. Then you begin to survey the evidence of how the various political parties address the issue of immigrants in their platforms and how politicians from the parties speak about immigrants in their typical campaign speeches and ads. This section of the paper lays out in a general way the evidence on which your argument rests. From this point on, you make your argument by making claims about the importance of the issue of immigrants in the political arena and then referring in detail to the evidence you surveyed in that section.

An outline reveals the structure of your paper and gives you a chance to tinker with it. It presents what you are writing about, what you have found through research, and what you have concluded about your subject. It will help you to step back from those details and consider the functional components of a paper. You can move topics around and make subordinate points into main points if you think the argument will work better that way.

The Functional Components of a Paper

Below is an outline of the working parts of a paper that tells what you should try to achieve in each.

Title Page:

Your title should be descriptive, not cute or mysterious. Sometimes your research question can serve as a title.

Introduction:

Introduce the topic: What is it, and why is it interesting or significant?

Provide background information: Orient your readers.

State the research question, implicitly or explicitly but clearly.

Discuss its significance by alluding to the controversy over the question: Why don't scholars or people agree on an answer? Sketch some different answers that have been offered and the arguments supporting them. Why would anyone ask the question in the first place? What difference will the answer make?

State your thesis.

Body of the Paper:

Make your argument: The argument must be made up of parts that follow from one another logically. Back up each element of your argument with evidence and discussion.

As noted in Chapter 4, you may consider challenges to your interpretation of the evidence or to your decision about what evidence is relevant (counterarguments) followed by your rebuttal. If you use counterarguments, address the way the evidence is used in them.

You may anticipate and refute possible criticisms of your argument: Doing this supplies counterarguments when other writers have not done it for you. However, do not make up a weak or outlandish counterargument. That is a called a "straw man," and it weakens rather than strengthens your own argument, because it makes the reader think that your thesis cannot stand up to a real challenge.

Note that you should occasionally remind the reader why your question is significant.

Conclusion:

In the conclusion you should merely affirm that your argument and handling of the evidence are persuasive. Do not introduce new arguments or new evidence; you should have made your argument in the body of the paper.

Expand on the significance of your argument (the "so what?"): How does your argument help readers to understand your topic better? Does your thesis lead to further questions that would not be raised by other theses? In general, what difference does your thesis make for understanding your topic and for future work on the topic?

Works Cited or Bibliography:

Give complete bibliographical information for every source you cite. This page provides a quick overview of your research.

Argument Chart

Here is another useful bookkeeping tool for organizing your paper. This chart will work well on the computer, either as a table or a spreadsheet, because you can add or delete rows as you develop your project. This model is based on a historical question about Florence during the Black Death. The "sources" and arguments do not reflect actual research; they are meant to suggest the kind of evidence and sources a person might use for such a project.

Question: What was the Florentines' religious response to the plague of 1348?

Working thesis: They disregarded the established church and created new religious groups, new rituals, and new ideas.

Argument	Evidence/Data
People stopped going to church.	Sermons indicating people were not going to church as they had before the plague. Accounts of popular preachers railing against the corruption of the church.
The plague generated new religious behavior.	Contemporary writers noted that laymen gathered in squares and marched in the streets, and they made up new prayers and rituals on those occasions. Contemporary accounts of penitential practices independent of the church, which claimed exclusive right "to bind and to loose."
Heretical views spread.	The Inquisition's records; letter from the bishop of Florence to the pope.
Boccaccio's *Decameron* shows that the plague drove people to abandon regular religious practices and to entertain dangerous ideas.	The *Decameron*

Explanation	Counterargument	Rebuttal
Sermons reflected concern of the clergy that the laity no longer trusted the church to protect it from God's wrath. People had regarded the church and traditional religious practices as protection against woes of the world (cite church lore about the efficacy of the Mass, prayer to the saints, and celebration of saints' days). The rise in the frequency and virulence of complaints about the corruption of the church suggests that people were disenchanted with the church.	People stayed away from church out of fear of getting the disease. Calls for reform of the church also predated the plague and had not previously affected attendance at church.	Perhaps, but the sermons do not attribute the empty churches to fear of the plague but to disenchantment with the church. Sources indicate that these calls increased in number and volume during the plague, indicating that people connected the corruption to the failure of the church to protect them from the disease.
Church did not protect the population from the plague. Description of new practices from the sources. Description of processions of flagellants and other "extreme" penitents (cite documents and secondary sources on the growth of these movements and their independence of the ecclesiastical hierarchy).	Popular religious practices outside the church predated the plague.	Popular religious practices had existed beside traditional, ecclesiastical religion. It matters that during the plague people turned to popular, nonecclesiastical practices instead of to the church. The scale of nonecclesiastical religious practices is new. Some new practices were introduced (such as processions of flagellants).
New judges were appointed to the Inquisition, indicating that it became more active. The number of cases the Inquisition heard doubled in 1349 from 1347. The bishop warned the pope that heresy was becoming a big problem in the diocese of Florence.		
The ten young people who escape from Florence to an isolated garden (Eden) meet in a church, which no longer can meet their perceived needs. The characters have lost their understanding of the divine moral order as taught by the church.	The *Decameron* rests on old models of story collections and cannot bear the weighty interpretation given to it here; it is a work of literature, not history or theology.	Boccaccio's introduction, properly understood, shows that he had more in mind than telling 100 stories. The intro. uses numerology to connect the framing story of the *Decameron* with traditional Christian ideas about the order of the world and the obligations of people.

Chapter 6

Using Evidence Properly
and Effectively

The proper use of evidence is the key to writing a good research paper. Good evidence, properly employed, not only supports your claims but also helps produce a coherent argument. But what kind of evidence does the thesis of a research paper rely on, how do you put evidence to work properly and effectively, and how much evidence is enough?

Directness of Evidence

In a research paper, you must use evidence to support your claims. But when a claim responds to a question selected specifically for its open-endedness—precisely the kind of question you want as a research question (see Chapter 3)—you naturally expect the evidence as a whole to remain inconclusive; for any number of reasons, a reader might draw an inference from the evidence that is different from the one you are urging. Yet the fact that you can't prove your argument does not mean that you can settle for making an argument that is less persuasive than you can possibly make it. On the contrary, it means you must argue your case all the more persuasively. One way to do so is by paying attention to the directness of your evidence.

The evidence you use will likely consist of many pieces. These can be classified according to whether they support your thesis directly or indirectly. Direct evidence for a claim is the kind of evidence that requires no inference in order to support the claim. What the evidence ostensibly shows it shows directly. If you needed to show when and where someone was born, a birth certificate with the seal of a secretary of state would be the most direct kind of evidence. At the other end of the spectrum might be testimony from a descendant whose information came from, say, an elderly great-uncle now dead for decades. Your reader would need to use inference to see such evidence as showing what it purportedly showed; in order to infer that the birth occurred when and where claimed, she would have to assume, e.g., that the great-uncle was in a good position to know what he is said to have claimed, that no misunderstandings occurred, and that faulty memories played no tricks over the years. Your reader could refuse to make these assumptions and infer on the contrary that the evidence did not adequately support the claim.[10] In between these extremes might be a document, such as a marriage license, that stated the age and place of birth of the person you are interested in. Such evidence would not be as direct as a birth certificate, but it would be a lot better than secondhand testimony. If the marriage license were consistent with the lore passed down in the family, and you knew that those testifying did not know about the license, then the case would be substantially strengthened.

Most of the evidence available to you will probably be indirect, yet you still need to assess its directness, in relative terms. In

---

10. As in the Western legal tradition, whose definition of direct evidence I have adapted for the purposes of this guide, the claim that a piece of evidence is direct is not to be understood as suggesting that literally no inference whatsoever is required to support the claim or that there can be no doubt about the authenticity of the evidence itself. Even the most direct evidence requires some inference. In the case of a birth certificate, one has to infer that the seal or the form represents an authentic state document. If the document were challenged, you would have to show that the seal or form did prove its authenticity, citing other evidence. The concept of direct evidence thus offers at best a handy tool for making a persuasive argument rather than a foolproof key to making a conclusive one. Yet it can prove useful when applied judiciously and with common sense.

In the history of law, until the 14th century, the courts accepted only direct evidence as probative. In criminal cases courts could only consider evidence from eyewitnesses or from those who themselves heard someone say something, such as a confession that he had robbed a church treasury. The idea that indirect evidence, called circumstantial evidence in modern law, could be used was first proposed in the middle of the 13th century but not accepted until much later. See R. M. Fraher, "Conviction According to Conscience: The Medieval Jurists' Debate Concerning Judicial Discretion and the Law of Proof," *Law and History Review* 7 (1989): 23–88.

assessing the directness of indirect evidence, you should judge
how much room a reader has for drawing inferences different
from the ones you want to draw and you should try to connect
pieces of evidence in ways that limit the reader's leeway to infer
something else. Your evidence as a whole should be as direct as
possible so that a reader is extremely likely to draw the inference
you want her to draw.

Search for Direct Evidence First

Suppose that you are writing on a topic in 20th-century American constitutional history and formulate the following question:
"What was the most important legal foundation of the 20th-
century U.S. civil rights movement?" After doing some research,
you propose that the cornerstone of civil rights law was a footnote in Justice Harlan Stone's opinion for the Supreme Court in
a 1938 case dealing with milk substitutes—the Carolene Products case. (Chief Justice Charles Evans Hughes is credited with
having suggested the inclusion of the footnote.) The relevant
part of the footnote reads:

> [The court need not, in this case, consider] whether preju-
> dice against *discrete and insular minorities* may be a special
> condition [that] tends seriously to curtail the operation of
> those political processes ordinarily to be relied upon to
> protect minorities, and which may call for a correspond-
> ingly more searching judicial inquiry.[11]

You cannot make the argument for your claim simply by saying that the language of the footnote outlines the kind of legal
reasoning that later civil rights advocates used—that is, that
when a law treats an identifiable minority, such as African
Americans, differently from others, the courts should scrutinize
the grounds for such treatment with special care. You have to
produce evidence. The most direct kind of evidence you can
produce is that later lawyers and judges used the actual footnote to make their arguments. This is the first kind of evidence
you should search for.

---

11. United States v. Carolene Products Co., U.S. Supreme Court, 1938,
304 U.S. 144.

Your research should lead you to the Korematsu case of 1944,[12] in which Justice Harry Black cited the footnote in dealing with the question of what standard of judicial scrutiny the courts should apply in reviewing the constitutionality of a federal law requiring the wartime internment of Americans of Japanese descent. Black's citation of the Carolene footnote is direct evidence of its influence, but additional evidence is required to demonstrate your thesis—that the footnote is the key legal foundation of the 20th-century civil rights movement. Further research should lead you to additional citations of the Carolene Products case in later civil rights cases, enabling you to trace a history of such citations in those cases and perhaps in the arguments of legislators considering civil rights legislation. Those citations constitute the main evidence supporting your claim. Yet you must also show that other plausible candidates for the title of legal cornerstone of the movement were not as important as the Carolene Products case footnote. You could treat the smaller number of citations you found in support of these other candidates as direct evidence that these other candidates were less influential than the Carolene footnote; in other words, you do not need to argue why a very straightforward comparison of the number of citations supports your claim about the greater influence of the Carolene footnote.

After exhausting your search for what looks like direct evidence, you should search for a less direct kind of evidence for your thesis. That search could consist of a comparison of the kinds of arguments used in 20th-century civil rights cases and might detect a pattern among cases in which the judge did not *cite* Carolene but nevertheless made the kind of argument *used* in Carolene. Such evidence is indirect. If it were all you could find, you would be making your argument from evidence that your reader could interpret as showing the influence of cases other than Carolene. But when you combine this indirect evidence with the direct evidence represented by the citations of the Carolene footnote, you increase the likelihood that your reader will see it as you do, as a confirmation of the significance of the Carolene case. In many cases, indirect evidence is the only kind one

---

12. Korematsu v. United States, U.S. Supreme Court, 1944, 323 U.S. 214.

can find to support a thesis, but search for any direct evidence, or evidence you think a reasonable reader would see as direct evidence, first.

Remember what constitutes evidence. If you are writing a paper based on primary sources—such as surveys, government databases, or historical documents and accounts—your evidence will come from those sources. The interpretations of scholars, taken from secondary sources, will not constitute evidence— of any kind—to use to support your argument. Rather, those opinions help you understand the evidence, give you insights, and perhaps lead you to additional evidence or suggest new ways to interpret evidence you have found. You cite them for the assistance they give you and in order to associate yourself with or disassociate yourself from their interpretations. However, if you are writing a paper about scholarly views of a topic, as is common in courses in sociology, anthropology, and political science, then the works of the scholars are your primary sources and their interpretations are your evidence. In such a paper, you seek to characterize and explain the work on a topic, and you cite the interpretations and opinions of scholars as evidence that supports your characterization.

Determining the Validity of Evidence—and Showing It

Evidence counts for nothing if your reader sees it as invalid, and a minimal criterion by which scholars judge the validity of a piece of evidence is its relevance—the extent to which it relates to the claim it purportedly supports. For example, a reader is not likely to consider crime statistics about Helsinki, Finland, as relevant to a claim about crime in Los Angeles. Evidence can be useful even if it is quite indirect, but data judged by your readers as irrelevant is never useful. Occasionally it may be difficult to judge whether a piece of data should be considered relevant; if you can't demonstrate or state a concrete reason for the relevance of a piece of evidence whose relevance may be doubted, don't use that piece.

In the example of the historical influence on American civil rights cases of a footnote in the 1938 Carolene Products case, the relevance of the footnote itself appears obvious because the footnote deals explicitly with the protection of minorities. However, if you could not show that later judges cited the footnote, its relevance to the history of civil rights law, and in particular its relevance to the claim that it was the legal cornerstone of the civil rights movement, would be greatly reduced, perhaps even extinguished.

You often have to argue for the relevance of evidence or show it by presenting other evidence that supports its relevance. And though you should not spend time searching for indirect evidence until you have convinced yourself that there is no direct evidence or no additional direct evidence to be found, there can be good reasons for choosing to *present* indirect evidence or evidence that is not clearly relevant before presenting direct evidence or clearly relevant evidence.

Suppose that, along lines of interpretation similar to those suggested in Deborah Solomon's *New York Times* review of R. Tripp Evans' biography of Grant Wood,[13] you offer the thesis that Wood's painting *American Gothic* was inspired by rituals associated with mourning. As evidence for your claim, you adduce the painter's close personal and professional association with the mortician David Turner. It is not obvious that this evidence is relevant, though it is plausible that it is. Yet, plausibility is not enough; you must offer evidence for its relevance. You point out that in the painting the curtains in the windows of the house behind the couple are drawn in broad daylight—a mourning custom in 19th- and early 20th-century America.

In itself, what we might call the curtain evidence constitutes indirect evidence for your thesis; after all, other explanations might account for why the curtains are drawn. But the curtain evidence, which accounts for a specific detail of the painting in a way that supports your thesis, is more clearly relevant to your thesis than the evidence of Wood's relationship with the mortician. Evidence of the relationship doesn't by itself provide much support for the claim that the painting was inspired by mourning rituals. Yet together the two pieces of evidence create a web of corroboration that greatly strengthens the case for your claim. Because the curtain evidence

---

13. Deborah Solomon, "Gothic American," review of *Grant Wood: A Life,* by R. Tripp Evans, *New York Times,* October 28, 2010.

is consistent with and coheres with the mortician evidence, it supports the relevance of the mortician evidence, while independently providing a relatively persuasive piece of evidence for your thesis.[14] Had you discovered a letter by Grant Wood suggesting that mourning rituals inspired the composition of the painting, that evidence would have been highly relevant to your claim—even if Wood did not specify how he used the rituals.

However, determining or showing that a piece of evidence is relevant to the thesis is not a sufficient condition for establishing that a piece of evidence is valid; validity also requires that evidence be reliable, or sound, and sometimes it is necessary to *show* that a piece of evidence and its use are sound. In the humanities, this means, roughly, showing that the evidence is based in fact and has been represented fairly. If you treat a painting purportedly by Vermeer as direct evidence for a claim about his work, you still have to argue that the work really is by Vermeer. Scholars have discovered many forgeries attributed to Vermeer.

The soundness of a piece of evidence depends on the quality of the source from which it comes. You can often take for granted the reliability or soundness of sources produced by a reputable agency, such as the U.S. Census Bureau, but not when dealing with the the kind of anonymous sources historians sometimes use. The authority of such sources stems from their age and relationship to the persons, events, or period they provide information about, but you have to show that the relationship is authentic. In a research paper, you will ordinarily do this by

---

14. In the example just given, presenting the clearly relevant curtain evidence before the less clearly relevant mortician evidence would eliminate the need to show the relevance of the mortician evidence: the identification of an apparent mourning symbol—and a rather powerful one—in the painting itself would make it obvious why the artist's relationship with a mortician is relevant to the thesis. But presenting the curtain evidence *after* the (questionably relevant) mortician evidence not only helps you weave a web of corroboration, it could give your reader a kind of "Aha" moment—an experience of illumination in which it suddenly "all makes sense": by being presented second, the clearly relevant and relatively persuasive curtain evidence appears to clinch the persuasiveness of, rather than merely cohere with and establish the relevance of, the less clearly relevant mortician evidence.

referring to the scholarship that has dealt with the quality and character of the source, but you may find that scholars differ in their views of the source and that you have to explain why you think one position is stronger than another.

Historians often face various other questions about the soundness and adequacy of evidence, because they use evidence from sources that happened to have survived—often not intact—the many processes of decay and destruction to which archives and libraries are vulnerable. A historian may have an undated document that she wants to use to support an argument, but the date matters. A dated document that quotes or refers to the undated one provides a "date-before-which" for the undated document; that is, the quotation of the undated document in a dated one shows that the undated document was issued or written before the dated one. An earlier, dated document that should have but doesn't cite the undated document might provide a "date-after-which" for the undated one; the failure of the author of the dated document to quote or cite the undated one strongly suggests that the undated document was issued or written after the dated one. In such a case, the historian may argue that the undated document can be dated with reasonable accuracy. How compelling a reader judges the undated document to be as evidence will depend in part on how persuasive she finds the historian's dating of it. That, in turn, will depend on whether she regards as convincing the claim that the earlier, dated document should have cited or quoted the undated document.

When sociologists and political scientists use surveys or databases as evidence, the question of the soundness of evidence takes on an additional methodological meaning; these scholars have to show not only that the data has been represented fairly but also that it was *collected* in such a way as to permit an accurate measure of whatever was supposed to have been measured. Showing this could consist in arguing that the survey questions were phrased so as to produce responses that can be taken as clearly expressing the subjects' views on a particular issue, or that the sample size or statistical technique conforms to accepted norms in the discipline. Databases also must be used with careful attention to issues regarding collection and representation. Do the "fields" in the database present the data in a way that permits one to use it to support the argument one wants to make?

It is not uncommon or inappropriate to use a good deal of space in a research paper to argue that a document, a picture, a story told by a contemporary, a database, and so forth, constitutes valid evidence for a claim you are making. You give reasons why this piece of evidence is valid as well as why it supports your answer to your question, while another piece of evidence is not valid and cannot be used by you or anyone else in a discussion of your topic. You'll find as you read scholarly works that much scholarship concerns questions of which evidence is relevant and sound and that the way a scholar answers these questions determines the answer he gives to his research question.

Putting Evidence to Work: Weaving a Web of Corroboration

Once you have assessed the relevance and soundness of the evidence you've collected, you have to use your evidence effectively. As we saw in the *American Gothic* example above, there are several ways to do so, but all involve corroboration or support— for claims, for other pieces of corroborating evidence, or for an argument in general.

As a model for how evidence might be used in a research paper as a whole, let's look at how it can function within one or two paragraphs of such a paper. A paragraph typically begins with a topic sentence, that is, a general statement of what the paragraph is about. In a research paper, the topic sentence will usually consist of a claim, such as "President Lincoln put off emancipation of the slaves because he feared that the border states, which were slave states that had stood with the Union in the Civil War, would join the Confederacy." This claim needs support, which is what the remainder of the paragraph should supply.

To provide that support, you might adduce one or more letters from the president himself that support the claim—fairly direct evidence for it. Yet using *only* those documents might allow a reader to raise questions, such as, "Did Lincoln's political purposes in writing the letter(s) lead him to present his views in a way that differed from what he actually believed?" So you might also cite the notes that one or more members of the cabinet took during discussions of the issue—evidence of a less direct kind, even if it appears to corroborate the evidence of the president's letters. Nevertheless, if you can cite two or three different pieces of evidence dated over several months to support your claim, you will present a strong case that your claim is true. Even though the evidence from the cabinet members' notes is less direct than the evidence from Lincoln's letters, the web of corroboration of which it is a part strengthens the claim about why Lincoln put off emancipating the slaves.

As seen above, a document cited to support the claim might require interpretation, because a reader might draw more than one conclusion about the meaning of the document as evidence. In other cases, a document's semantic meaning itself might be ambiguous. Both kinds of problems with evidence force you to defend your interpretation of the document, perhaps by citing other evidence. If you are using art or literary works or data sets as sources of evidence, then you almost certainly will have to explain or interpret what you have found; the meaning of those kinds of evidence is rarely self-evident or subject to only one interpretation.

Explanation and Interpretation of Evidence

What is meant in this context by *explanation* and *interpretation?* The two terms can be used almost interchangeably, but they denote different phases of the process of delving beneath the surface of the data, statements, or texts you are using as evidence in order to show the meaning of that evidence or to draw inferences from it. In Chapter 5 we saw how in the field of history (as in sociology, anthropology, and political science), a scholar's argument about the meaning of surnames in marriage could rely on statements that she treated as texts—things that had to be interpreted. In literary studies and art history, scholarship often relies in a similar way on a scholar's interpretation of the texts or artworks she is writing about. The thesis of such a study might consist of a claim to have identified a previously unnoticed or underappreciated aspect of a text or painting. The argument in support of this claim might show that certain words or elements of the text or painting appear simple but are in fact complex.

The introduction to Boccaccio's *Decameron* provides an example. The framing story of the *Decameron,* which is a collection of 100 short stories, involves ten young people trying to escape the ravages of the plague in Florence in 1348. The ten consist of seven women and three men. The introduction tells how they abandon Florence for a country estate where they spend ten days telling one another stories of love and adventure amid luxury and comfort. Boccaccio notes that the oldest of the young women was 27 in 1348. He tells us that the youngest was 18. Thus, the oldest was born in 1321 and the youngest in 1330.

A scholar familiar with medieval numerology who noticed these details might ask whether Boccaccio's citing of these ages had any theological significance. She might become persuaded that it did and that the author intended his readers to see his story as having a hidden meaning—specifically, that he meant to comment indirectly on the moral character of what the young people undertook to do.

To make an argument in support of this thesis, she might point out that the numbers 3 and 7 were symbolic numbers in medieval Europe, citing evidence that this was so. According to medieval commentators, three was the number of the Trinity and therefore of the spirit, while seven was the number of Man, because Man has a body made of the four material elements (earth, water, air, and fire) and an eternal soul of a spiritual substance. The composition of the group, seven women and three men, aligns with this medieval numerology. Then, she might point out that the birthdates of the two women whose ages Boccaccio gave added up to seven ($1 + 3 + 2 + 1 = 7$ and $1 + 3 + 3 + 0 = 7$). Moreover, their ages in 1348 were multiples of three, and the difference between their ages, nine years, was also a multiple of three. From this interpretation of the text, the scholar might conclude that Boccaccio wanted his readers to see that his story of dalliance had a cosmic significance; it was actually a story about the God-given moral obligations that people had—and might fail to uphold—in the face of the plague. The numbers and ages of the ten young people showed that they were abandoning not just Florence but their proper place in God's moral universe.[15]

---

15. Many scholars have proposed interpretations of the numerology of Boccaccio's framing story. For a summary of their views, see Joy H. Potter, *Five Frames for the Decameron: Communication and Social Systems in the Cornice* (Princeton, NJ: Princeton University Press, 1982), p. 75ff.; and Cormac O Cuilleanain, *Religion and the Clergy in Boccaccio's Decameron* (Rome: Edizioni di Storia e Letteratura, 1984), p. 83ff.

Data sets also require interpretation. If survey data reveal that large numbers of blue-collar workers, who had traditionally voted for Democrats, suddenly began to vote for Republicans in 1980, a political scientist should ask why. He might start by looking carefully at the data, seeking geographic patterns or fine distinctions between those who voted Republican and those who stuck by their old allegiances. Then, like the literary scholar, he might bring other evidence into the picture. He might suggest that certain economic and social changes, such as the growth of homeownership in some segments of the blue-collar workforce, or widespread layoffs in some industries, or exploitation by Republicans of cultural values—such as strongly supporting military spending or opposing abortion—led to the change. The scholar interprets the data by reading it with a magnifying glass while taking into account patterns, relationships, correlations, and anomalies, and explains it by arguing that certain changes in the circumstances of the blue-collar electorate or in the positions of the Republican Party caused the changes revealed by the data. To interpret and explain evidence is always to do so in view of the claim for which the evidence has been adduced, that is, the claim your argument supports.

What Is Sufficient Evidence to Support an Argument?

Some evidence may be necessary but insufficient to show the truth of a thesis. In the Carolene Products case example, it was necessary to show that the footnote was important in the history of civil rights litigation, and the argument proceeded by tracing a history of citations of the footnote in legal opinions and so forth. But in order to establish the claim that the footnote was the *most* important legal foundation of the civil rights movement, more had to be shown—that all other candidates for that title were less important. In this instance, seeing that the citation evidence for the Carolene footnote was, by itself, insufficient to establish the truth of the thesis was a simple matter of deductive logic.

Now consider some examples of a different and less straightforward kind. First, a scholar makes a claim and cites a document to support it. Readers look up the cited text and discover that he did not cite the relevant passage in its entirety but merely selectively. They may conclude that the scholar did not use the evidence fairly.

Second, a scholar makes a claim and cites a single sentence from a primary source as evidence to support it. There is no other evidence to cite. Readers may judge that there is not enough evidence to support the scholar's claim.

Third, a scholar does 200 interviews for a study. In her published study, she reviews the interview process, gives statistics on the interviews, explains the way the questions were asked, and then asserts, explicitly or implicitly, that the particular interviews she cites in making her argument are representative of the survey as a whole. If her peers think that she interviewed a sufficient number of people and that she has provided enough information about the overall results of her interviews, then they are likely to agree that she has used her evidence properly. There is enough of it, and it is fairly treated.

In cases where insufficiency of evidence can be deduced as a simple matter of logic, it is easy enough to tell when you must say more. But in most cases, there is no hard and fast rule to guide you in deciding when you've said *enough*. To say that you need just enough evidence to be convincing or to make your case is not much help. So try to put yourself in a skeptical reader's position and imagine what sort of and how much evidence would persuade such a reader that your argument is sound. By constantly asking how much evidence is enough you will keep in mind the need to explain both the evidence and your principles of selection, so that your reader does not second-guess you. The explanation of how you have used the evidence is also an argument that you've used it fairly and that as far as you know there is no other evidence that is relevant to or would alter the answer to your question.

You want to construct a persuasive argument. An argument that ignores some of the evidence will collapse and bring you and your ideas down with it. An argument that cites too much evidence often obscures the points you are trying to make; your reader cannot tell what your argument stands on. Novice writers commonly want to cite every bit of information they found during their research. They did all that work and want to show it off. But an argument loaded with a superfluity of evidence becomes repetitive, tedious, and sometimes digressive, leading to discussions that have nothing to do with the thesis being argued.

Such an argument becomes unpersuasive, because superfluous

evidence can create the impression of special pleading. The appearance of special pleading makes the reader suspicious and unlikely to follow you when you reach those places in your argument where you may have to use phrases like, "It is not unreasonable to conclude that"—that is, where you are urging that an inference be drawn on the basis of evidence that is admittedly inconclusive.[16]

If you are selecting evidence to cite from a large mass of material that you've discovered, you must explain to the reader why you think the evidence you've selected is sufficient. Such an explanation will consist in arguing both that what you've selected is representative of the material you did not cite, and that it is sufficient to prove your argument. The explanation is an argument that you have used the right amount of evidence in the right way—that is, that you have not left out information that would support a thesis different from yours and have not taken quotations or "facts" out of context.

In general, you need to persuade your reader that you have not used the evidence just to make your argument come out the way you wish—in other words, that you have based your thesis on the evidence, not the evidence on the thesis. If, putting yourself in the position of a critical reader, you think you have used the evidence fairly and ethically, then you probably have.[17] If, as is often the case with politicians, ideologues, and interest groups, your answer to your question has become more important to you than the evidence you've found to support it, there is a strong probability that you will not have used the evidence fairly or persuasively.

---

16. You could put some of the extra evidence you have found in a footnote, where it will not overload your argument or confuse your reader. However, you should be careful not to add too many footnotes containing material and comments that are unnecessary to your argument, because your reader may start to pay less attention to your notes than you want him to.

17. Note, however, that the use of quantitative, including statistical, analysis requires special training, as does the ethical use of data derived from research on human subjects.

Chapter 7

Using the Work of Others: Crediting Your Sources

Placing One's Work in the Context of Earlier Scholarship

As you do research, you will notice that in professional scholarship the author nearly always begins with references to the work of earlier scholars and then says that those works raise additional questions or give an inadequate answer to the question he or she will deal with in the article or book. Such beginnings are not merely conventional but intrinsically related to the primary aim of scholarship itself: the building up of shared knowledge. You cannot contribute to the edifice of knowledge without being familiar with the work of earlier scholars and aware of how your work relates and is indebted to work done by others.

In all research projects you will gather the findings and opinions of others who have gone before you. Remember that the hallmarks of academic writing are the explicit recognition of the place of your project and your thesis in the tradition of scholarship on your topic and the demonstration of how you arrived at your thesis. That's why plagiarism, using someone else's ideas or words without attribution, is such a serious offense. It subverts the very nature of academic work. Moreover, it is now almost impossible to get away with plagiarism. If a student can find something on the Internet, so can a teacher, and there are several very effective online services that match the texts of papers against both huge databases of old papers and the Internet as a whole. It is far better to take the consequences of a failure to get the work of research and writing done well—a low grade—than to end up with an F and a note on the transcript indicating that the F resulted from plagiarism or some other form of cheating.

Using the Work of Others

You will use the work of others in several ways:

- You will borrow **passages** from others' work—that is, you will quote them or paraphrase their words. You must cite such sources precisely, usually in a footnote or endnote. If you are quoting, use quotation marks. There are several styles of citation—each discipline has guidelines—and your instructor will usually specify which one you should use. However, every style of citation provides complete information about the source somewhere, in the footnote or endnote itself or in the bibliography, to which the notes refer. The information should include the name of the author, the title of the work from which the passage comes, the place of publication, the name of the publisher (or if a journal article, the name of the journal), the date of publication, and the page on which the passage can be found.

- You will use **sources** used by others or brought to your attention by others. In the case of primary sources, you must acknowledge that you learned of these sources from such and such a scholar, citing the place where he or she published it or cited it in the same way as you would cite a quotation from the scholar. In the case of secondary sources, where a scholar's footnotes or bibliography have suggested further reading in the scholarly literature, you usually do not have to cite the source of your knowledge when you use one of those works. In rare instances, however, you might tell your reader that you were led to a particular secondary source by a citation in another work of scholarship. An example of such an instance would be one in which the source was unusual because it appeared to deal with a different subject and you would never have found it had a particular scholar not pointed it out and suggested its relevance.

- You will borrow **ideas or even arguments** from others. You must cite the author from whom you got the idea. Often, a proper citation will have not only a plain citation to the book

or article and page number(s) where the scholar expressed the
idea but also an explanation of the way the author used the
idea. The explanation can be especially useful if you are using
the idea in a way that is different from the way its originator
did. Then your careful citation will help your reader distinguish your ideas and contributions from those of your sources
and help your reader give you credit for what you've done.
For example, if you are citing a text that Jones used in her
work but you are using it in a different way, you would refer
to the text in your paper and then add a footnote of this sort:
"Cited in Jones, *Title,* p. 101 [full bibliographical information
would have been given in an earlier note or in the bibliogra-
phy]. Jones cited the text to show that 12th-century lawyers
did not regard Martinus [a Roman lawyer in the service of
Emperor Frederick I of Germany, r. 1152–90] as correct in
his analysis of royal power over the property rights of his subjects. However, the text, dated to the early 13th century, also
illustrates the way Frederick I was thinking about his newly
acquired imperial authority."

Quotations can be formatted in various ways according to type
and purpose. The most significant type of quotation is that of
text on which you want to comment. Usually, such quotations
are several lines long and are set in a separate, indented block of
text within a paragraph. For example, if you were writing about
Emperor Frederick I's conception of imperial power, you might
quote a decree of the Diet he held at Roncalgia in northern
Italy in November 1158 like this:

> The prince possesses all jurisdiction and all coercive power.
> All judges ought to accept their administration from the
> prince.

In a footnote after the quotation, you would cite your
source—perhaps, "From the first decree of Roncaglia, trans. by
K. Pennington in *The Prince and the Law* (Berkeley: University
of California Press, 1993), p. 14." You would then proceed to
interpret the text. What does "jurisdiction" include? What does
it mean that only the prince has coercive power? Does the text
imply that judges are agents of the king, rather than independent
arbiters? The text is an object of study. You want your reader to
look at it with you. If you were writing a paper on art history,

the object would probably be a painting or sculpture, which you would reproduce in your paper. You want your reader to be able to refer to the object as you discuss it.

If you are making an argument based on a text, such as the Bible, a tract or literary work, or a legal document, you might quote a small piece of text as evidence that supports your position. For example, if you were arguing that St. Paul held that Christians did not have to obey the law of the Old Testament, you might quote his letter to the Galatians, "For you [the Christians] were called to freedom [from the law]" (Gal. 5:13). You put such a brief quotation into the sentence in which you refer to it.

Sometimes, you want to use just a few words of a source, because their author has expressed a pertinent idea in so distinctive and useful a way that you cannot do better. Doris Kearns Goodwin's description of Abraham Lincoln's cabinet as a "team of rivals" is an example. When you use a phrase, credit it in a footnote even if you have acknowledged the source in the text: "As Doris Kearns Goodwin expressed it, . . ."[18]

Some uses of quotation marks have nothing to do formally with the quotation of another's words. One is the "scare quote." Scare quotes are used, usually for individual words, in cases where it's useful to signal explicitly that a term—one's own or another's—is being used in an unusual way. Sometimes scare quotes indicate irony, as in, "The legislature introduced this regressive measure to ensure that the country remains 'the land of the free.'" (Note: Use single quotes when quoting within a quotation.) Sometimes they signal awareness of an inadequacy in the use of a given term in the context in question. In Chapter 3, on p. 38, you'll see scare quotes around the term "fact," an acknowledgment that what one treats as a fact is often a claim whose truth remains debatable, rather than a given like the date of the U.S. presidential election in 2008. Because of the ambiguity inherent in the use of scare quotes and the possibility that they may be confused with other uses of quotation marks, you should use them sparingly in research papers.

---

18. Doris Kearns Goodwin, *Team of Rivals: The Political Genius of Abraham Lincoln* (New York: Simon & Schuster, 2005).

Another use of quotation marks that has nothing to do with the quotation of another's words is that of drawing attention to a term *as a term*. For example: "Below you'll see scare quotes around the word 'facts'"; and "In this paper, the term 'middle-class' shall be defined as follows . . ."

Citations and the Authority of Your Sources

You must never use another's words without attribution, even if those words come from a source, such as Wikipedia, that appears to have no author(s) to credit. In research, it is always important to know and to be able to judge the authority of sources, because your own authority rests on the authority of your sources. The old warning for computer users, "garbage in, garbage out," applies equally to research papers, and secondary sources without identifiable authors are by definition garbage, because the reader cannot verify their accuracy, honesty, or scholarly standing. (As seen in Chapter 6, although great care must be taken to establish their reliability, you can sometimes use anonymous primary sources in research.)

Moreover, a great many writers of websites plagiarize. Many instructors have discovered that students who committed plagiarism by taking text from a website copied from plagiarizers. That might be amusing if the students didn't end up with permanent marks as cheaters on their records. Quoting from anonymous web sources, even with proper citation, does not provide useful evidence for your argument, because the "evidence" does not meet the standard of credibility. Finding the ultimate source of information taken from a website requires that you investigate the source of the source, a time-consuming task that might lead to layer upon layer of plagiarism before you find the source you can cite.

Giving Credit Is Essential to the Enterprise

There are many reasons for writing your own paper and crediting your sources, aside from fear of getting caught and suffering all the awful consequences of having the mark of a cheater on your transcript. The first reason, of course, is the moral one. It is wrong to plagiarize or to cheat in other ways.

The other reasons stem from the very nature of a research

project or paper. You lose nothing by citing the work of others properly. Indeed, by doing so you show that you are part of the tradition of scholarship in your subject, that you understand that scholarship, and that you are making an independent contribution to or judgment about the subject. By honoring those whose work you have used, you honor your own work.

There are other reasons to cite your sources. First, scholarship, including yours, rests on trust. You must trust that the work reported in the sources you use was honestly done. Without that assumption, one would have to start every project from scratch, and knowledge would not progress. We'd all be stuck at the first step, showing that early Parliaments spent most of their time on judicial cases, resurveying people about how they voted, or why they moved from one church to another. If you could not trust the honesty and competence of those who have gone before you, you could not use data without collecting and organizing it yourself. We all trust and verify, by asking some of the basic questions noted in Chapters 2 and 6, so that we can use what others have done. We cite the work of those on whom we rely.

Second, and following from the first point, scholarship is a group activity, even though some contributors worked decades ago. When you write a research paper, even as an undergraduate, you join that group. If you think of your project in that way, you can see that crediting the work of others is an essential component of your effort. A work group that does not acknowledge the contributions of all soon disintegrates. A plagiarist doesn't just fail to cooperate, he threatens the integrity of the group effort in which, supposedly, he was participating.

And engaging in an exchange of constructive criticism is also essential for group work. When you write a paper for a class, you can easily commit the fallacy of thinking that the objective is to produce a good piece of work and get a good grade; you can feel as if the enterprise is about you and your performance. Certainly, that is part of what is happening in a college course, but it will help you to think of your work as part of a larger effort to find the answer to some question that has interested scholars and students in the field for a long time. The exchange of criticism is part of the enterprise. You critique the work you read, and your instructor, who, like you, becomes a temporary member of the group when she reads your paper, criticizes you. Everyone learns from criticism, unless it is merely snarky. Good criticism is constructive; it starts from the notion that all of us are trying to make a serious contribution. Learn to give and take constructive criticism, which entails acknowledging the work of others while trying to advance the common project.

Finally, the work you do on research projects and papers is the core of your education. It is in doing such assignments that you learn how to make and use knowledge, which is what a person whose career requires an education does. An educated person knows how to use sources of information, how to construct a sound argument, and how to assess the evidence that supports it. She thinks for herself and knows and acknowledges when she is making an original contribution as opposed to a simple report of what others have done. This capacity requires that one be able to judge one's own work, to hold it at arm's length. Distinguishing your ideas and discoveries from those of others—your sources in a research paper—demonstrates that you are becoming an educated person.

Strategies for Avoiding Misuse of Sources

To credit the authors you have read properly, you must keep excellent bibliographic records as you do your research (see Chapter 2). Always start by recording complete information about the publication—author, title, and so on. Then, record the page number of every note you take from that source. If you keep good records, you will minimize the possibility that you will use another person's work without attribution, and you will save a great deal of time when you sit down to write your paper. You will not have to go back to the library to look for the source of quotations or information that you want to use.

To prevent yourself from inadvertently using another writer's words, do not copy text from your sources directly into your notes without marking the passage clearly—usually with quotation marks—as a quotation. If you just copy the sentences or phrases into your notes, you are unlikely to remember, when you finally get around to using the information in your paper, that they are not your words. The best way to avoid using another writer's words without attribution is to avoid copying text verbatim into your notes. If you put the book or article you are reading aside or turn it over before you make your note on it, you help ensure that you are actively recasting the idea in your own words. You must still note the bibliographic data identifying where you got the information or idea, but you probably won't have to worry that you are inadvertently quoting someone without proper attribution.

A last bit of advice related to plagiarism: Make and keep versions of your paper as your write it. Until students acquired computers, they used typewriters for writing. They typed a draft, revised it, and retyped it. If they were very conscientious about their work, they might produce three or four drafts before typing up the final version, and all of the versions would be thrown into a manila folder. The computer has changed the writing process. You draft the paper and revise it electronically, producing a clean, continuously evolving copy that absorbs each stage of your writing. For most students, this process produces only a single version, the final one, which they print up and hand in. Avoid ending up with one version of your paper; create drafts— paper 1, paper 2, and so on, by saving versions as you proceed through the process of writing and revising.

Years ago, in the typewriter era, a student handed in a paper to me that was so good I suspected that it had been plagiarized. I could not find a source, but I called the student in and told him that I suspected plagiarism, because the paper was so much better than the first written assignment I had received from him and than one would expect from an undergraduate. I asked if he could show me how he produced the paper. The next morning, he showed up with five drafts of the paper. After I had given him a hard time about the first paper, he had been determined to show me that he was really good. The drafts showed that he was really good. He got an A+, and my everlasting respect, which did him some good when he asked me for a recommendation to graduate school.

When you complete a draft of your paper on the computer, save it and revise a copy. If you go on to a second revision, do the same. Label the version you hand in so that you can identify it later if you need to. This practice will not only produce a folder of drafts as evidence of your work, but also save passages that you deleted in the course of revising. One often decides that a deleted passage was good and relevant after all; it is convenient to have it saved in an earlier version of the paper.

Chapter 8

Shaping the Paper: Writing a Prospectus and a Rough Draft

Once you've organized your materials, you are ready to write a rough draft. Sometimes, you will be required to write a prospectus before you create the rough draft, and sometimes you will find it useful to write a prospectus as a way to prepare yourself for writing the rough draft. You approach both a prospectus and a rough draft in the same way, so the two will be treated together.

It is at the point of writing a draft that many writers bog down, uncertain about how to proceed. The outline discussed in Chapter 5 or the worksheet at the end of this chapter will help you get started. You can use a worksheet in any of the following ways:

- As a template for writing a prospectus, if your assignment asks you to provide one or if you think it would be useful to you as a starting point for writing your draft

- As an aid in solidifying your argument, helping you to see what its "moving parts" are

- As a guide for structuring your rough draft

- As a tool for evaluating your rough draft during substantive revision

The Value and Character of a Prospectus

A *prospectus* is a very brief summary of your paper. A *rough draft* is a first attempt at actually writing the paper. Thus a prospectus is almost like an outline, except that you write out your question, thesis, and arguments in full sentences. **The advantage of writing a prospectus, as opposed to an outline, is that the**

process of writing one is an excellent tool for formulating your argument. When you write out your arguments, you formulate them, making it easy to study them. A written argument can be an object of study in a way that an unwritten one, or a sketch as in an outline, cannot be.

You may think that writing a prospectus is a waste of time, but it can help you develop your paper in several ways. You can think of a prospectus as a proposal for a paper, an attempt to convince someone that you have come up with a good question, have a coherent and sound thesis, have found good and sufficient evidence, and can make good arguments in support of your thesis. If you don't have to turn in a prospectus, then the person you are writing it for is yourself in your role as critical reader. In one to two pages, the prospectus makes a case that you have built the foundation of a good paper. The prospectus gives you an opportunity to assess the way you are expressing your ideas. Is the question phrased well? Is your thesis coherent? Are you able to express the essence of each of your arguments clearly and concisely? Do you have a good idea of what evidence will support the various components of your argument? A prospectus gives you an overall view of the paper and the clarity of its various parts. In addition, it should make it much easier to write the rough draft.

Writing a Rough Draft

When you write your rough draft, make it longer than the target length of the final paper. That means you should put into it most, if not all, of the material you have found through your research. The relevance or usefulness of some of the material you have read while doing research will have been clear when you were structuring your argument, but if there is any question about whether something will help or hinder your argument, keep it until you can see how it works in your rough draft.

You want your first draft to be "fat," because in revising it to produce your second draft, you want to eliminate rather than add material and arguments. If you add new material when you write a second draft, you will not have a complete second draft. A second draft that contains significant new material is a mixed draft. Some of it has been honed and improved over the rough draft; some of it is just as rough as what you started with. The point of writing a rough draft and then editing it is to hone your argument—tighten it, improve your use of evidence, get rid of extraneous material, assure that the argument flows logically, smooth the transitions from one point to the next, and so forth. If you have added significant new material while revising your rough draft, then you've gone back to the first stage of your writing and have to start the revision process over again. If you just go on without starting over, your final paper will not be as good as it could be.

Using a Rough Draft Worksheet

In the writing program that underlies this guide, students receive the rough draft worksheet printed below. Use the worksheet to prepare for your prospectus or rough draft.

- **As a prospectus template:** Fill in all of the blanks on the worksheet. Use the completed worksheet as a rough outline for writing your prospectus. A prospectus is usually a 1- to 2-page summary of your paper. In it you set out your question and thesis, outline your argument and the main counter-arguments, and indicate what kind of evidence you have to support your argument. One way to think about a prospectus is as an explanation of your project to your instructor. If your instructor insists on approving paper topics, then you need to make a presentation about what you propose to do. The instructor will want to know your question, your working thesis, the outline of your argument, and the kind of evidence you expect to use. The judgment about the appropriateness of the project will rest on his view about whether your question is worth investigating, whether your working thesis is plausible, whether it looks like your argument, if you make it, can support your thesis, whether you will use the right kind of evidence, and whether you can finish the project in the time you have. Even if the instructor does not want such a presentation, for some people writing a prospectus is a good first step toward writing a rough draft.

- **As a guide to solidifying your argument:** Fill in as many blanks on the worksheet as you can. If there are any blanks that you cannot fill, take it as a sign that your argument has some weak spots. Review your notes or do more research until you can complete the worksheet.

- **As a guide for structuring your rough draft:** The worksheet's elements are arranged in the order in which they might typically appear in a research paper. The first part of the worksheet—the topic, question, alternative arguments, rebuttal, and statement of the thesis—corresponds to a paper's introduction. The next section constitutes the body of the paper, advancing the different parts of your argument, each part accompanied by supporting evidence, scholarly opinion, and explanation. (Note that while the worksheet has three spaces for specifying the evidence on which your argument rests, this arrangement is not intended as a recommended structure for your paper. Your argument will not necessarily rest on three pieces or bodies of evidence. The worksheet only gives you an idea of the order of your paper, not its content.) The final section, on the significance of your thesis, constitutes a crucial part of the conclusion.

- **As an evaluative tool during revision:** After you have written a complete rough draft, make sure that it contains at least some material that corresponds to each element in the worksheet. Go back to your notes or do additional research to fill in the gaps and to strengthen underdeveloped areas.

The Rough Draft/Prospectus Worksheet[19]

In my research on the topic of _____

_____

I have learned the following: _____

_____

_____

These observations lead me to pose the following question: ___

_____

_____

This question has several plausible answers. For example, scholars

such as _____

and _____ have claimed that _____

_____

It is also possible to argue that _____

_____

[add more if necessary]

_____

19. Used by permission of the Making of the Modern World program, Roosevelt College, University of California, San Diego.

While the above answers are plausible, they have several weaknesses. These weaknesses include: _____

_____

_____

_____

My own answer to the question (my thesis) is as follows: _____

_____

_____

_____

My thesis is supported by the following piece of evidence: _____

_____

_____

(*Reference*: _____)

My thesis is also supported by: _____

_____

_____

(*Reference*: _____)

My thesis is further supported by: _____

_____

_____

(*Reference:* _____)

[*add more if necessary*]

My thesis is significant because it modifies and/or adds to current thinking on this topic in the following way: _____

_____

_____

_____

Chapter 9

Revising the Rough Draft

When you revise a rough draft, you should aim for substantive changes—improvements in organization, the logical flow of the argument, and the use of evidence. During this revision, you will almost certainly need to make substantive sentence-level revisions as well, but you should spend as little time as possible on the most meticulous kind of sentence-level revision—polishing your prose—for two reasons: first, focusing on grammar and style during this revision will make it difficult for you to see where you need to make substantive or structural changes; second, fine-tuning sentences that you might ultimately decide to amend or delete will waste time. You should therefore save polishing your prose for the next stage of revision.

The Goals of Revising a Rough Draft

At this stage in the process, your goals will be to:

- Organize the main sections of your paper to make your argument as persuasive as possible; the argument should march through the paper.

- Strengthen the organization within each of your paragraphs.

- Delete redundant or extraneous passages.

- Delete redundant or extraneous words and phrases. (In general, you should write as tersely as you can. By tightening your prose, you will move your argument and your reader along.)

- Note where you need to do additional research.[20]

- Make sure that your paper has an explicitly stated thesis and that each paragraph contributes to the argument that the thesis is sound.

- Make sure your paragraphs flow logically from one to the next.

- Make sure that your conclusion and your thesis match up; that is, make sure that the main point of your conclusion is the same as the point of the thesis you advance in your introduction.

- Make sure that you have cited your sources properly. As noted earlier, your instructor will probably have assigned a style manual that specifies how you should cite works in footnotes. If not, you have two choices. You can give full bibliographical information about a work the first time you cite it and then use abbreviated references to it in subsequent notes, or you can say in your first note that you will give abbreviated references in the notes that direct the reader to the full bibliographical information in the bibliography or list of works cited. In the first style, the first time you cite Woodward's book on the new South, the note would read: "C. Vann Woodward, *The Origins of the New South, 1877–1913* (Baton Rouge: Louisiana State University Press, 1951), p. 101." The second time you cite the book, you could write, "Woodward, *Origins,* p. 115." In the second style, you would put the full bibliographical information in the bibliography, and your footnotes would read, "Woodward, 1951, p. 115."

  You should use footnotes, not endnotes. Word processing programs automatically adjust the organization of a page to accommodate footnotes, so it is unnecessary to send the reader to the end of the work to find references. A note should be where it best supports your argument or statement, and that is at the bottom of the page.

---

20. Obviously, at this point in the process you are unlikely to have time to do extensive additional research, but you may be able to fill some gaps in your evidence. If you do add material, be careful to look at the additions again. They are in first-draft condition, while the rest of the paper has reached the second draft.

Organizing the Paper

Number the paragraphs of your rough draft. On a separate sheet of paper, make a numbered list in which you write one brief sentence summarizing the main point of each of your paragraphs. Some word processing programs will list first sentences of paragraphs automatically. Using such a feature is unwise. The point of making the list is for you to focus on the topic sentences of your paragraphs, which you can do best by writing them out yourself.

Analyzing the list will help you improve the organization and flow of your paper. In particular, you should do the following:

- **Make sure that each of your paragraphs has only one main idea.** If you find that you cannot easily summarize a paragraph, it probably makes more than one point. (Just as a sentence should express one idea, each paragraph should present one point of your argument.) If necessary, divide paragraphs into two or more shorter paragraphs.

- **Eliminate redundancy.** If you find that two or more paragraphs contain the same information or make the same point, combine that information into one paragraph or a smaller number of paragraphs—preferably one.

- **Make sure that all the material related to a single point is in the same place.** If two or more paragraphs address the same topic or main idea, make sure that they are in the same part of the paper, moving them if necessary. Don't discuss a topic in two different parts of a paper; at the very least, don't discuss the same topic in two different parts of the paper *in order to make the same point.* Try to treat each topic completely and then move on to the next topic. If necessary, refer to an earlier discussion or remind your reader that you have already argued a point, but don't divide your discussion of a topic.

- **Look at where you have placed each of your main points.** Your argument will be most persuasive if you place your strongest point last, your next strongest point first, and all other points in the middle of your paper. Move paragraphs around if necessary. However, the governing principle of your organization should be the logical progression of your argument, and, if arranging the argument into an order for rhetorical effect breaks up or undermines its logic, favor the logic over the effect. Generally, an argument that flows logically will be persuasive, so long as the evidence supports it.

- **Look at where you have placed counterarguments and rebuttals.** Remember that whatever comes last in your paper will have the strongest effect; for that reason, make sure that counterarguments are not in either the last or next-to-last paragraph. Counterarguments and rebuttals are more effectively placed after the introduction or within the body of the paper, as appropriate.

Chapter 10

Copyediting and Final Revision

Experienced writers know that there is no limit to the number of times one can revise a piece of writing. In fact, the one and only rule of limitation in revising a paper is:

When it's due, it's done.

Final Revision

Final revision takes place in the last day or two before you hand in the paper. Remind yourself that you cannot rewrite your entire paper in that amount of time, no matter how many flaws you think you have found in it or how much new evidence you have just discovered. If you have stuck to a strict writing schedule, you will have already completed your substantive revision—for organization, presentation, and effective use of evidence—by the time you need to edit and polish your paper.

What follows is a very brief and incomplete list of problems to look for in your writing as you go through the paper for the last time. There are many guides to good writing, and you were probably required to buy one for your first composition course. It will be a much better guide than the one provided here. None of the following suggestions is meant to be a hard-and-fast rule, but paying attention to them will improve your writing and make you aware of your tendencies as a writer. Good writers know the rules of grammar and style, and they break them when doing so will produce clarity or a desirable effect in the reader (a smile, a grumble, a recognition).

To improve the clarity of your writing, do the following:

- **Avoid overuse of "to be" verbs** ("is," "are," "was," "were," "have been," etc.)

  Before: "The most frequent reason why Protestants move from one denomination to another <u>is</u> a change in marital status."

  After: "Most often Protestants move from one denomination to another because of a change of marital status."

When you use a form of "to be" in a sentence, you are writing an equation: something equals something else. Sometimes that is exactly what you want to do, but in most instances such sentences slow the flow of your argument and "deactivate" it. Here, note how much more forward-moving the *After* sentence is than the *Before*.

- **Use the active voice rather than the passive voice**

  Before: "The <u>animosity</u> between medieval Muslims and Jews <u>is underestimated</u>."

  After: "<u>Modern historians underestimate</u> the animosity between medieval Muslims and Jews."

Note that using the active voice allows you to specify who the *actors* are: that is, who (in the example) has underestimated the animosity. So active sentences often provide more information than passive ones.

- **Make sure that the referent of each word such as "this," "these," "those," "it," and "they" is clear**

  Before: (The first sentence of a paragraph) "The message of empowerment that <u>they</u> projected through their writings supposedly encouraged other women to do the same. Yet <u>this</u> was not the case. For <u>these</u> women, it was not a form of empowerment. It was a source of escapism. <u>These</u> are poignant reminders of how women looked to escape from the hardships of life."

After: (The first sentence of a paragraph) "The message of empowerment projected by the work of 19th-century women writers encouraged other women, their readers, to do their own writing. Yet 19th-century women did not write diaries with the aim of empowering others but as an escape from their own everyday burdens and constraints. The masterpieces they left behind poignantly remind us how they sought to escape the hardships of their lives."

The original passage suffers from, among other things, not only the use of ambiguous adjectives ("For *these* women"—for *which* women? the writers? their readers? both?) and pronouns ("*it* was not a form of empowerment"—*what* was not a form of empowerment? the writing? the reading? both?) but also an over-reliance on the verb "to be."

• **Tighten your prose further**

Before: "This shows how important it was for Muslims to acquire knowledge, no matter where they had to look for it. This was characteristic of Muslims. Throughout their conquests in various regions of the world, they adopted scientific and technological knowledge from their neighbors. As a result, the Muslims acquired different forms of knowledge from various cultures and civilizations without concern for the way such knowledge might challenge their beliefs." (68 words)

After: "The above verse demonstrates Muslims' indiscriminate desire to acquire knowledge. As their empire expanded Muslims absorbed scientific and technological knowledge from many cultures without concern for the theological challenges such knowledge might pose." (32 words)

As noted in the last chapter, you should tighten up your argument and prose when you revise the first draft for substantive change. The example above should have been revised for conciseness in that first revision. At this final stage, you are polishing your prose, but looking for any remaining unnecessary words and phrases is part of that process.

- **Cut pairs of nouns and pairs of adjectives** when one noun or adjective would suffice. In the last example, note "cultures and civilizations"; these terms have similar but different meanings as well as different connotations. Choose the one that best reflects your intended meaning.

- **Avoid verbs made from nouns.** Many verbs that end in "ize," such as *prioritize*, are made from nouns (*priority*). Some of these verbs, such as *legitimize*, have been fully absorbed into the language and are fine. Others are new formations and will not look right to readers. They also may not have a completely settled meaning. *Priority* means being earlier in date or superior in rank; *prioritize* usually means putting a group of things in order, but that meaning is not consistent with the noun it came from. In general, you do not want your reader to focus on your choice of words but on your choice of meaning. Don't trip up the reader with new, trendy, not-quite-clear words.

Final Suggestions

As you go through your paper, don't try to do everything at once. Instead, concentrate on one (or maybe two) aspects of revising on each read-through. For example, you might highlight all the "to be" verbs and then try to transform many of them into active verbs. Or you might locate all instances of the passive voice and revise those sentences into the active voice.

One of the best things you can do is to read your paper aloud; because the ear is less tolerant than the eye, you can often identify infelicities easier by reading aloud than by reading silently.

Revising is a repetitive process. You go through your paper several times, concentrating on one writing issue after another. Each of these passes through the paper should go quickly.

Final Revision Checklist

- Revise for clarity.

- Revise for subject-pronoun agreement and subject-verb agreement.

- Use your computer's spell-check.

- On a hard copy, double-check for spelling errors that the spell-check software won't catch (that is, any typographical error that is a real word but the wrong word for the sentence).

- Make sure that each of the authors you cite in the body of the paper is included in your "works cited" page and that each of the authors listed under "works cited" has at least one reference in the body of your paper.

Conclusion

If you complete the process described in this guide, you will produce a paper you can be proud of. In addition, you'll learn and practice intellectual skills that will serve you in everything you do in school and after you've left school. You are getting a college education because you want to make your way in the world using your intellect. The essence of intellectual work is using knowledge to find things out and to persuade others that your conclusions are correct and your arguments sound. You learn to use knowledge by doing research papers.

You are not in school merely to learn facts but to learn how to *use* facts—that is, to learn what facts are and how they can be marshaled to formulate and support ideas. When you've learned how to formulate a research question, to do research to answer it, and to construct an argument to support your answer, you have learned the most important skills college can teach you. And you'll do superior work in school and in whatever profession you enter. You came to college with intellectual potential. Projects like the one outlined in this guide will turn that potential into high achievement and the ability to succeed in your chosen work.

Index